R U Assertive?

R U Assertive?
Stand Up Skills for Teenagers

Gloria Hash Marcus

HALSEY
PRESS

Copyright @ 2015 by Gloria Hash Marcus
No part of this book may be used or reproduced in any manner whatsoever without written permission.

For information regarding this book write to:
Halsey Counseling and Educational Center
Attn: Gloria Hash Marcus
330 East Coffee Street
Greenville, SC 29601
or call (864) 527-5910
www.assertiveskills.com

ISBN: 978-1-943290-03-1
Library of Congress Control Number: 2015948098

The content of this book is not intended as a substitute for professional services. The reader may need to consult a counselor, psychologist, psychiatrist, or other mental health provider for professional services. This book is provided with the understanding that the publisher is not rendering legal or psychological services.

The names of clients or any information that would lead to their identity has been changed to protect their privacy.

For simplicity, I have referred to clients in pronoun form as "he" and "his."

R U ASSERTIVE? STAND UP SKILLS FOR TEENAGERS was first published and printed in 2005.

Contents

Introduction for Teenagers 1

Introduction for Parents 3

1. What are Assertive Skills? 5

2. What Communication Styles are not Assertive Skills 21

3. Techniques for Knowing Yourself 31

    Space Cushions 31

    Boundaries 33

    Drawing 39

    Writing Sprints 44

    Breathing 46

    Relaxation Exercises 48

4. Self-Knowledge Leads to Self-Advocacy 51

5. Learning Disabilities, Dyslexia, AD/HD and NLD 69

6. Extreme Social Situations 89

7. Additional Self-Support Techniques 95

    Fogging 95

    Broken Record 97

    Positive Self-Talk................................ 100

    Positive Pictures in Your Mind................... 104

    Conflict Management 106

Conclusion... 113

Additional Practice Exercises 115

References 127

About the Author 129

Introduction for Teenagers

This book is for you. It is about growing stronger in yourself. It is about taking care of yourself, knowing what you want, and speaking up for yourself. It is a book about new roads, new paths that you can take, new ways of living that may be more satisfying for you.

Read the book and try the exercises. Change requires work. Practice. Be patient with yourself as a new and stronger you emerges.

If you are a teenager ask your parents to read this book. If they do not have assertive skills, ask them to learn assertive skills and to help you practice these skills. Good communication skills will help you and your parents grow closer. In many ways assertive skills can smooth out relationships with family members, as well as help you meet your goals and needs. Assertive skills will support you in not having to guess or wonder in your mind what the other person meant; you will not have to interpret what is unspoken, unsaid. You will begin to ask questions that will clear up what you want and what you need to know.

If you are a teenager who has a learning difference or who has Attention-Deficit/Hyperactivity Disorder (AD/HD) this book can help you understand your symptoms and develop better coping strategies.

Introduction for Parents

How have we gotten off track in our ability to communicate with each other? I am writing this book because assertive skills are techniques that can be very beneficial in helping your teenagers navigate these important years in their lives. The power of this skill carries over to adulthood. When your child is confronted with the first cigarette or enticed to cheat on a major test, how will he respond? If your child has not been taught how to recognize what he feels and how to speak up for himself, the moment will come when he may collapse because he may not have the words to carry him through the stressful situation. Even with assertive skills there are no guarantees that your child will take the right course, but without assertive skills there is less hope of being able to carve out a space that clearly defines who he is and speaks to what he wants to happen.

There is power in fostering your child's interests and sense of self. All of our children are seeking significance, competence, and power. These psychological states are more readily attainable if we support our children in knowing who they are and by supporting them in learning to speak for themselves. Identity formation comes from a knowledge and understanding of who we are. Once we begin to develop a better understanding of ourselves, we must learn to make use of that self information with assertive skills.

I frequently ask parents of my clients, "Are you going to college with Sam?" "Are you going to raise Sam's children?" The parents then have a puzzled look on their faces and say, "No, oh no." I then ask the teenager and the parents how they are going to navigate the child's transition to adult years when their teenager is not clear regarding his feelings, how he feels about issues, or how to speak up for himself. Assertive skills consist of powerful communication tools that demand that our teenagers know themselves and speak up for themselves. There is power in having an adult foster the unique interests and a stronger sense of self in teenagers.

Teaching assertive skills should begin around age six when a child begins to be "other" focused. At six years of age, identity formation is proceeding and a child realizes that the world involves more people and many different life situations. There is a world of emotional negotiation and mediation that lies ahead. This is a great age for helping a child begin to identify what he feels and to learn how to appropriately and adequately express those feelings. If the foundation of self-knowledge is begun at an early age, it is a natural progression for the child to build on assertive skills as he enters more challenging teenage years. Knowledge of self and techniques in communication skills will continue to give benefits to your child. Once this knowledge of self and communication skills are taught, self-growth continues to be fostered. Your child will have the gift of having a stronger sense of self and be more prepared for dealing with peers, school, and life challenges.

Chapter 1
What are Assertive Skills?

Assertive skills are ways of communicating that allow you to identify what you want and to give words to your desires. The use of assertive skills can be thought of as basic to your happiness. Why? It is you who knows yourself best and who is responsible for giving a voice to what you want and need. In this chapter you will learn what assertive skills are and how you can become more assertive in all areas of your life. You will review the four types of communication styles and develop stronger skills in identifying what you want and how to express those needs. You will also learn about roadblocks that may interfere with your use of assertive skills. There are exercises along the way to help you identify and sharpen your skills.

What are assertive skills? Assert means (1) to state positively; affirm; declare or (2) to maintain as a right or claim, with words. To assert oneself means to put forward and defend one's own rights or claims. To use assertive skills means that you know yourself and you speak up for yourself. You speak from a place that is true for yourself. You express your needs, your wants, and your desires. Using assertive skills does not mean that life will be rosy and that you will get all that you ask for, but you will come closer to meeting your goals and desires if you know what they are and give voice to them in an appropriate manner. Assertive skills are useful in regular, daily activities and in larger decisions that you have to make in life. They can be as insignificant as asking your mom to buy you a new shirt, or as significant as standing up for yourself and saying "no" when you are asked to cheat on an exam.

You may think that you are born knowing assertive skills. You are not. Assertive skills are a way of speaking up for yourself. In order to have assertive skills, you must be in touch with what you want or how you want something in your life to be different.

Communication Styles

There are four different styles or methods of communication: aggressive, passive, passive-aggressive, and assertive. The style that is the most effective is called assertive. The assertive style is more effective than the other types of communication styles because assertive skills come from a place of ownership or knowing what you want. You are speaking for yourself and are balancing the skills that involve taking care of yourself and communicating with others. Assertive skills involve balance because you are in touch with what you want or need and are sensitive to the rights and well-being of others. The other styles of communication— aggressive, passive, and passive-aggressive—are often used, but may not have the positive outcome that you want. Here are examples of each style of communication:

Assertive

You say:
I need money for the dance Friday night, can you help with this?

or

I want to go to the movies this weekend with my friends. Is that OK?

What Are Assertive Skills?

Aggressive

You say:
You are an idiot.

or

I hate you and I want you to die.

or

You are stupid and can't help me finish this assignment.

Passive

You say:
I can't go to the dance Friday because Mom won't give me any money (and you haven't even asked her). or Sarah will never go out with me, so I am not even going to ask her and see what she might say.

Passive-Aggressive

You say:
I'll hurt my brother because my parents will not let me go out Friday night to the dance. (Perhaps these are thoughts that are not spoken).

or

I'll talk out and disrupt the class because I made a 63 on the math test.

or

I'll take his lunch box and hide it because he won't let me copy his homework.

The Assertive Style

In assertive skills **intent** or **motive** is very powerful. Your intent or motive is the desire or thought form behind your words. A student can politely request, "May I have $3.50 for lunch money?" and the tone can be one of a respectful request. Or, a student can be demanding with similar words and fiercely state, "I need $3.50 for lunch money!" This may communicate being pushy, demanding, and a lack of respect.

What is the difference in these two requests? The words are both the same but the **attitude** of the speaker and the **feeling** of the words is quite different. The tone of the words and the delivery of the words completely change the content of what is being said. You are no longer using assertive skills when your intent is to be demanding, pushy, or to run over someone else. This is an example of aggressive skills, and it is not assertive.

To assert means to speak, to voice what you think and feel. One of the simplest ways to be assertive is to start a statement with an "I" message. An "I" message means that you begin the sentence with "I" because you are stating a need, a want, or a desire. Examples include the following: "I want to go to the movies today." "I need more lunch money." "I'm upset about my grades," etc. These are fairly simple statements. It may be more challenging to assertively state your needs when they are more emotionally involved such as the following: "I'm not happy about how I've been treated in this relationship." "I wish that you would hold my hand this way." "I am uncomfortable when you are that close." "I don't like the way you responded when I asked if you could tell me where you were last night." "I need an HIV test."

What Are Assertive Skills?

"I" Messages

"I" messages bring out the best reaction in interacting with others because when we use "I" messages we take responsibility for ourselves, our feelings, and our desires. When we use "I" messages we are taking care of ourselves; we are stating an outcome that we hope can be reached.

Here is a simple formula for practicing "I" messages:

I _____ (state what you feel)

_____ (behavior)

because _____ .

(how this could affect you)

For example:

I   <u>am frustrated and need some help</u>
with   <u>my math course</u>
because <u>I made a D on the last quiz</u>.

I   <u>am upset</u>
when   <u>you don't keep your promise</u>
because <u>I feel that I do not matter to you</u>.

I   <u>am happy</u>
when   <u>you purchase football tickets</u>
because <u>it makes me feel like you care about me</u>.

9

I	*can't understand*
how	*to clean my room*
because	*I never seem to please you with how I fix it*.

Remember to state what you need from the other person.

Roadblocks to Assertive Skills

What makes having assertive skills so difficult? You may not have adequately learned how to listen to yourself, to know what you truly want, or how to communicate with yourself or with others. One reason that you may not be assertive is that you may be removed from your true feelings. You may be distant from your feelings. Knowing what you want may be more complicated than listening to yourself. It may be difficult to identify your thoughts, feelings, and desires. You may not know how you feel—so you can't verbalize your thoughts or feelings. Although knowing what you want may be challenging, when you do know—you often don't use your knowledge—because you may not know how to go forward, how to assert yourself.

In their book *The Anger Control Workbook* (2000) Matthew McKay and Peter Rogers state that "I" messages should be fair, reasonable, and friendly. Being assertive does not mean being demanding, pushy, or necessarily getting what you want. Instead, it means that you have taken care of yourself by clearly stating your needs or desires. It is as though you have built a protective, invisible wall around yourself that says, "I care enough about myself to ask for what I believe myself to be worthy of, to be deserving of." Remember, it is as important to be assertive in small, daily matters as it is to be in more significant and life-changing situations.

To be assertive means to be worthy, to feel deserving of stating your thoughts and feelings. What makes you worthy? You are worthy because you exist. You are worthy because you are reading these words. You have equal worthiness to the most well

What Are Assertive Skills?

known person on earth or to the richest person in the world. The world tells us that there are degrees of worthiness, but this is not true. We all have value; we are all worthy of getting in touch with our true feelings and expressing them.

> I worked with a teenager in private practice who for several years at bedtime "tucked her parents in at night." She lived in fear of telling her parents that they could hire someone to do this, that it wasn't her place, that she did not want to do this, etc. But she was afraid that her parents would "fall apart."

Fear of speaking up is one of the biggest roadblocks in using assertive skills. It was fear that kept this teenager from speaking up about her true feelings about not wanting to "tuck her parents in at night." However, as you read about this situation, you may think that it is ridiculous and you may ask yourself why this student did not speak up. The truth of the matter is that there may be many situations in your own life that you are afraid to deal with and are afraid to let others know how you truly feel.

You may be afraid of expressing your true feelings for several reasons. You may believe that if you assert yourself, someone will be hurt. However, that kind of thinking is confusing aggression with assertiveness. Remember, to be assertive is to know and state your needs and desires, while to be aggressive is to attack someone verbally or physically. You may not want to speak up because you may have a passive communication style. To be passive is to deny your right to speak up, to give up having a voice. Some clients have told me that they feel selfish or guilty when they use assertive skills. Assertive skills may be a form of "healthy" or "enlightened" selfishness. As you develop and grow emotionally, it is important to learn that **you must take care of yourself**. This is part of your responsibility to yourself; care-taking of you is not selfishness. It is important to know and state what you want. Remember, others cannot read your mind. It is you who must speak up for yourself. Also, you may need practice in identifying what you want, as well as in learning how to speak those words. Moreover, taking care of yourself in a balanced way—by using assertive skills—should not make you feel guilty about yourself. Using assertive skills will help strengthen your emotional self.

As was stated earlier, one of the easiest ways to begin practicing assertive skills is to begin a sentence with an "I" statement; then, your thoughts should follow. Simple "I" statements include the following examples:

- I need to go to the store to pick up some construction paper.
- I want to go to Sam's party tonight.
- I am upset about the way you yelled at me last night.

When your parents ask you why you haven't begun a project and you don't know how and where to begin this project, you may use the following assertive statements:

- I am unclear about what to do.
- I feel overwhelmed with this project.
- I don't know where to start.

Body Language and Assertive Skills

Learning assertive skills increases the odds that you will have more self-respect and a greater sense of power and freedom in your life. This occurs because:

- You express your feelings and needs
- You take responsibility for yourself

Here are some examples of body language that may be helpful in using assertive skills:

1. Face the person
2. Make eye contact

What Are Assertive Skills?

3. Stand or sit tall and straight (get support from your body)
4. Notice the physical distance between you and the person you are addressing
5. Be relaxed (tension makes things worse)
6. Speak clearly
7. Listen to the tone of your voice. Are you calm? Angry? Hurt? Resentful? Steady? Prepared?

If you feel unsteady, practice in front of a mirror, with your dog, with a friend, etc., *before* you communicate your thoughts.

Role play these situations:

- Someone you know asks you to go to a party where drugs and alcohol will be served.
- A classmate asks you to steal when you are in a store shopping.
- A "friend" wants to plan with you how to cheat on an exam.
- Your brother asks you to lie for him about where he is spending the night.
- A classmate tells a teacher that you were cheating on an exam and you were not.
- A classmate says that they saw you "cheating on your boyfriend" and you did not.

R U Assertive?

Practice Exercises

Remember the formula for stating "I" messages:

I _____(state what you feel)

_____(behavior)

because _____.

(how this could affect you)

Read the following and practice writing "I" statements.

The following "I" statements involve problems that you are having with your friends:

I was upset when I was not invited to your party.

I think you were flirting with my boyfriend and I want to know what was going on.

I don't understand why you don't call me anymore.

Write three additional "I" statements about problems that you may be having with your friend.

_____

_____

_____

What Are Assertive Skills?

When you are asked to use drugs these "I" statements may be useful:

I am afraid I will get in trouble. I am not going to break the law.

I need all the brain power that I have. I can't afford to loose any more gray matter.

I'm not old enough.

I don't have extra money.

Write three additional "I" statements about not using drugs.

_____

_____

_____

These "I" statements may be useful if you are asked to cheat on a test:

I work hard for my grades.

I can't do that.

I want to stay in school.

I don't need to be suspended.

I just better not.

Write three "I" statements that you could use when asked to cheat on a test.

_____

_____

_____

R U Assertive?

"I" messages do not necessarily involve problems. It is important to be assertive in our everyday conversations. For example, the following "I" statements convey appreciation:

I appreciate you sharing your iPad with me.

I like it when you listen to me and I am probably not making any sense.

I appreciate you for giving me a ride.

I appreciate you taking time out of your schedule and mowing the lawn for me.

List three positive "I" statements.

_____

_____

_____

Assertive skills are not going to develop immediately. You must be willing to practice. If you can be assertive when you are **not** under stress, you will be much more likely to be assertive when you are faced with a challenging situation.

Practice Exercises

Practice saying and making up your own "I" statements for the following school situations:

    I don't understand this assignment.

    I need help with problems 45 through 51.

    I need extra help; where can I get that?

    I let myself down with this grade; what can I do to improve?

Add three assertive "I" messages for school situations.

_____

_____

_____

Remember **intent** is more powerful than your words. If you are just talking and pretend to really care—but you don't—others may feel the emptiness of your words. If your true desire is to improve yourself that will also come across. If you use assertive skills to gain something and you are not being genuine or honest, you may not have the outcome that you desire. If you are not true with your words your teachers, your parents, your friends, etc. may know and so will you—and the outcome may not be what you wanted. Again, assertive skills do not guarantee a certain result in your life.

If you are not being honest with yourself in stating your needs, others will not know what you feel and want. Other people may know that you are not coming from a place of truth within yourself.

When you get discouraged in learning and in practicing how to communicate, remember that you are precious; you are worthy of knowing yourself and stating your needs. We are all worthy.

Practice Exercises

Write three examples of assertive skills when you can't complete your homework.

_____

_____

_____

List three examples of assertive skills when something goes very well.

_____

_____

_____

Write three assertive statements for asking your parents to let you go to the movies Saturday night.

_____

_____

_____

Write three assertive statements for asking an employee in a store for help.

_____

_____

_____

What Are Assertive Skills?

Write three assertive statements for asking a teacher for extra help.

_____

_____

_____

Write three assertive statements for asking a teacher why you made a certain grade.

_____

_____

_____

Write three assertive statements for asking your parents to do something for you (i.e., take you out to eat, take you to the movies, play basketball with you, etc.).

_____

_____

_____

Chapter 2
What Communication Styles are Not Assertive Skills
Aggresive
Passive
Passive-Aggressive

Now that you know what assertive skills are, it is also important to recognize communication styles that are not effective. These ineffective styles of communication—aggressive, passive, and passive-aggressive—block your ability to express your needs and interfere with your ability to get your needs met. In this chapter you will learn to identify ineffective communication styles that prevent you from being an assertive teenager. You will learn to recognize the difference between assertive and non-assertive communication styles and learn how you can improve your ability to get your needs met.

The following are examples of communication styles that are not assertive skills. They represent forms of communication that will not serve you well.

A. Aggressive

Aggressive communication styles involve attacking others with your words. You may state your needs in a way that is aggressive, abusive, and hurtful. If you say, "You don't know what you're doing," "You really blew that project," or "You are stupid," you are being verbally aggressive. To be aggressive is to make personal your comments to another person. This may possibly cause harm to another. It may not be a visual, noticeable harm, like physically hitting someone, but we inflict harm and pain with our words just as though we were hitting or injuring someone. When you are aggressive with your words you may also cause harm to yourself.

Rather than say "I am upset about my chemistry grade. . .," you may state, "Mrs. Brown is a stupid, incompetent teacher." The prior remark is aggressive because the student deals with his emotions by verbally attacking the teacher. Another example of being verbally aggressive may involve communication with your parents. Rather than, "I hope you'll let me go to the dance Friday," you state, "My parents are idiots, like dinosaurs, and never let me do anything. They never listen to me."

When you are aggressive with your words you may cause emotional or psychological hurt and harm to another person. You may have less chance of getting what you want. Your unkind words may come back to you, and you may end up hurting yourself. It is important to note that there are occasions when you may be aggressive because you do not know how or what you truly feel. You may become overwhelmed with emotion, can't sort out how you really feel, and may lash out at someone you care about because you are so emotionally strung out.

B. Passive

Passive communication styles involve knowing that you want or need something, but doing little or nothing about it. When you are passive you may not ask for what you think you want or deserve. You may not feel good enough about yourself to believe you are worthy of asking for things or of having your needs met. With passive communication there is also the possibility that you do not act because you do not know what you really want. You may not speak up for yourself because your awareness of what you want is clouded, not clear. So, there are several reasons for exhibiting passive behavior: you may not know what you want; you may feel unworthy of asking; you may have grown up in a house where family members were not taught to speak up for themselves, etc.

If you have a passive communication style you may become self-pitying; passive people may become "victims." You may unknowingly feel that everyone has power over your life—except you. Inside you may think, "Poor me, I never get what I want." "I don't deserve an 'A.'" "I don't deserve a good spot on the basketball team," etc. "I can't believe that Jonah would pick me for his girlfriend—I wonder what he wants." Perhaps one of your parents is passive, and you have not been exposed to a parent who is assertive and asks for what he wants or states his needs. An example of passive communication skills is when other students ask you what you want to do on Friday night and instead of stating your true wants, i.e., to go to the football game, you say, "What do you want to do?" or, "Nothing really matters to me." Then everyone agrees to go to a movie but you don't like the movie, and you're not happy at the movie. Why would a student be passive in this situation? Why would this happen? Perhaps you did not feel worthy enough about yourself or you did not know yourself well enough to state what you truly wanted.

Perhaps you were afraid the other students would make fun of your idea, maybe you did not really know what you wanted to do on Friday night, or perhaps you felt that your opinion did not matter. Maybe you are not as popular as other students, and you feel it is not your place to speak up. Regardless of why you didn't state your real feelings, what you said comes back to trouble you because you feel "cheated." You feel less than everyone else; you do not feel "okay" or "worthy." Perhaps you feel left out or left behind.

C. Passive-Aggressive

Passive-aggressive communication styles are another example of not using assertive skills. To be passive-aggressive may involve a lack of self-worth or an anger that is thinly veiled. In passive-aggressive states you may not acknowledge or "own" what you want, what you truly desire, or what you need. As a result of this, you are angry. One difference between passive styles and passive-aggressive styles is that a passive-aggressive style has an extra aspect of being angry, but not being truthful about your anger. With passive-aggressive communication, you may ask for things in a roundabout fashion. You do not have the skills to be direct and you are angry.

An example of passive-aggressive skills is when you get mad at your teacher because you just learned that your final history grade of 68 meant that you failed the course for the semester. In an anger that is not open or honest, you put nails in front of the tires of the teacher's car at the end of the school day. You are furious with the teacher but not honest with yourself or your anger. You misdirect your anger. You don't "own" your anger.

Behind passive-aggressive statements and passive-aggressive actions is an anger at others, and more importantly, often an anger to yourself. Where does that anger come from? Perhaps you were raised in a family that taught you that anger is not okay—that having anger or angry thoughts makes you a bad person. Anger is like all feelings that we have discussed. Anger is not "good" or "bad." Feelings are not "good" or "bad." Do not put labels or judgments on feelings such as "good" and "bad."

What Communication Styles are Not Assertive Skills

They are just feelings. What gives feelings direction and power is what you do with them.

It's okay to be angry; however, it is not okay to go out and shoot someone because you're angry. It's okay to be frustrated about your chemistry test grade; it's not okay to cheat. It's okay to be jealous of Sam's new car; however, it's not okay to steal a car or to damage another car.

Do you get the picture? You may be afraid of your feelings because you believe that having a feeling such as anger makes you an angry person. This is not so. Having a feeling is very different from demonstrating that feeling and expressing it. I once heard that it is difficult to control your thoughts and even more difficult to control your feelings, but you **can** control your actions.

I once had an adult babysitter who told me that she didn't care what my four-year-old son felt; she just wanted him to do what she said. I have always tried to teach my children to acknowledge what is in their hearts and minds and to express it verbally. That babysitter came to our house just once. She was more interested in making my son obey her than in recognizing his worth as a four-year-old. I am not saying that it is okay for children to be disobedient; however, I am stating that my four-year-old son was worthy of his opinion, his ideas, and his thoughts. Although I am a strong disciplinarian, what she was saying to my son was, "Listen to me, I am an adult, I have power over you; your thoughts and your feelings don't matter." This upset both my son and me very much. I've always tried to convey to my children, "You are beautiful and worthy of being heard ... your father and I are in charge ... but in this home, in our world, your feelings are worthy of being heard and expressed."

Using another example of passive-aggressive communication, a student may be angry at the teacher, but may decide to take his anger out on the teacher—by not studying, by not completing assignments, or by poor attempts at work. This is misdirected anger—the aggressive part of passive-aggression. The passive aspect involves the student not clearly identifying his feelings or needs and not speaking up about them. In this situation the student is causing harm to himself and not to the teacher.

If you grew up in a punitive household or in a controlling home, you may spend a significant amount of time trying to second-guess your parents, trying to interpret what your parents wanted. You may grow more distant from your true feelings and desires. As time goes by, you may not know who you are or what you want. When there is a blur between your sense of self and the self of your parent, enmeshment has occurred. Enmeshment means that you are emotionally entangled with someone else. The boundary lines between who you are and what you want and someone else and what he wants are no longer clear. You may begin to unknowingly "speak" for another person, and not represent your "true" self. You may not realize that you are sacrificing a self-knowing for an "other pleasing." Your parents may have fostered or encouraged this psychological position and may believe that you will grow into a fine adult. This may not come true. You may be safe as long as your world is predictable. However, you may be at risk for folding or collapsing under peer pressure because you have not learned who you are and what you want. You may know how to please mom and dad at the expense of not knowing and not taking care of yourself, and thereby develop an incomplete sense of self. You may seek to please others in life, sacrificing your own sense of self as well as the ability to recognize and assert your true desires.

In reviewing assertive skills and nonassertive styles of communication (i.e., aggressive, passive, and passive-aggressive styles) consider the following script and decide on a healthy response: Your teacher made an assignment for the class to complete a project by February 25th. You forgot to write down the assignment. The date comes and you don't have work to turn in. If you were assertive, you would go to the teacher and clearly state that you forgot to write the assignment in your agenda. Is there any way that you can make up for the mistake? If you used an aggressive approach you may speak badly about the teacher directly to her. If you were passive, you might do nothing, get a

What Communication Styles are Not Assertive Skills

zero on the report, and hope that you can hide your report card from your parents. If you were passive-aggressive, you might write a cruel note to the teacher, not sign it, and put it in her box in the teacher's lounge. Which method is most effective? Which method would support and take care of you? Which method is the most effective style of communication?

All four of these responses represent ways of communication, ways of dealing with a situation. However, only one response obtained a good outcome. One student exhibited assertive skills by stating his needs through "I" messages. Are you beginning to see that assertive skills are a process of taking care of yourself in your speech and actions? As you use more and more assertive skills you will gather strength by "being true to yourself" and by taking care of yourself.

Let's work on styles of communication. Label each of the statements in the chart on the next page. At the end of this exercise explore your thoughts on your responses.

R U Assertive?

	Assertive	Aggressive	Passive	Passive-Aggressive
You don't know what you're talking about.	___	___	___	___
You aren't fair to me.	___	___	___	___
I need a book from the store to complete my project.	___	___	___	___
I failed the math test, and I give up on this subject.	___	___	___	___
If she won't help me I'll forget to feed her cat.	___	___	___	___
I'll return my library book late because it is closed.	___	___	___	___
If you loved me, you'd let me buy that prom dress.	___	___	___	___
I feel like I wasn't included in the family vacation.	___	___	___	___
I want to go snow skiing Saturday.	___	___	___	___
He took my CD player so I'll break his radio.	___	___	___	___
Mom won't let me stay up tonight so I'll use a flashlight to finish my computer game.	___	___	___	___
My friend didn't invite me to her party so I won't vote for her to be head cheerleader.	___	___	___	___
I'll let him cheat on my paper so I'll be on his team in PE.	___	___	___	___

What Communication Styles are Not Assertive Skills

Examples of aggressive statements include the following:
- You are stupid.
- You are a loser.
- You are an idiot, a jerk.

List three aggressive statements.

_____

_____

_____

Examples of passive statements include the following:
- She spoke badly about me and it must be true.
- They say I'm a poor runner and I guess I'll have to quit the team.

List three passive statements.

_____

_____

_____

Examples of passive-aggressive statements include the following:
- She didn't ask me to her party, so I'm going to tell lies about her to her friends.
- Mom and Dad won't let me go to the movie with my friends, so I'll take their car without asking.

R U Assertive?

List three passive-aggressive statements.

_____

_____

_____

Aggressive — She's an idiot!

Passive — I can't ask her to the dance. Nobody would go out with me, especially her!

Passive Aggressive — I'll get them back for not inviting me, I'll egg their house!

Match each statement with the correct communication style:

Aggressive (A)   Passive (P)   Passive-Aggressive (PA)

___You are a stupid seventh-grader, what do you know?

___I can't get a date for the dance, so I won't go.

___He won't let me cheat off his test, so I'll throw something in class and let him get blamed.

___You're a loser and can't get a date for the prom.

___Your dress is so pretty (then tells other students it must have come from the thrift store).

___I don't know what we're talking about in class, so I am not going to even try and study for the test.

___He didn't invite me to his party, so I'll paper roll his house.

___You are a loser face.

___Your Mama is . . .

Chapter 3
Techniques for Knowing Yourself

Now that you are learning how to speak up for yourself with better clarity, you will be more likely to use these assertive skills if you develop more knowledge about yourself and others. This chapter is designed to help you develop this self-knowledge by teaching you techniques for taking care of yourself emotionally in a variety of situations. These techniques will help you define who you want to interact with and how you want to define your relationships to other people in your life. As a result of using these techniques, you will become more self-aware and self-assured. As you increase your self-awareness and self-assurance, you will grow stronger in your ability to assert yourself.

We shall now explore six techniques that will help you learn about yourself.

Technique #1: Space Cushions

In private practice I often teach clients that they take up the space with which they are familiar (their bodies) and they also take up another space around themselves that I call their "space cushion." What is your space cushion? It is the nonphysical space around you. It is the air that surrounds you. To learn about your space cushion do the following exercise: stand about 15 feet apart from another person and develop eye contact with the person you are facing. After you have made eye contact, ask him to walk toward you. As he walks toward you, think of your personal comfort zone. That is the space where you are and where you feel "OK." In other words, it is the space that you actually take up and the space around you where you feel comfortable. As the person walks toward you, hold your arm out with your hand extended and say "stop" when you are no longer comfortable. Then look at the space that remains. This is your "space cushion." It is a space that you occupy which is very similar to the space that your body occupies. Your space cushion is just as important as the physical space that your body requires. This is an exercise in knowing yourself because once another student, a teacher, etc. enters your space cushion, you may feel irritable or unsettled simply because someone you don't like has entered your space. Your space cushion also changes based on your feelings toward the person who is in your "zone." If someone whom you are very fond of enters your space cushion, you may be pleased, happy, and want him to come closer. But if someone with whom you have had an argument enters your space cushion, you may bristle and want more distance from that person. Only you can know your space cushion. Your space cushion may change from day-to-day, and it can also change from morning to afternoon or even hourly.

Practice knowing your space cushion. Are there occasions when you want physical distance from your peer group? When do you want others to be close to you? Notice the line in the grocery store or at Wal-Mart. Do the people in front of you have large or small space cushions? How much distance is there between customers in the store? Do you feel uncomfortable if you get close to someone in line who has a large space cushion?

A client of mine who was having trouble with her brother took this exercise a step further and explained that her trouble with her brother was that he was in "the space cushion of my mind." What a graphic way of knowing that someone is in your head and you don't want that person in your mind—at least not right now.

Technique #2: Boundaries

Boundaries are what define you. Boundaries involve your physical being as well as your nonphysical space. Boundaries tell you where you start and stop. Boundaries are lines that you draw around yourself that help you define who you are. Boundaries help you define what you are taking in and what you are giving out. Some boundaries can be seen and others can not. Boundaries develop from a sense of who you are, and are shaped by your desires, your limitations, your emotional flexibility, your belief system, your hurts, your pleasures, etc. There may be times when you are uncertain about your boundaries because you may have some confusion about what you want. A lack of self-knowledge or self-awareness can create difficulty for you. If you don't know yourself, you may have difficulty with boundaries. You may not know what you truly want. You may have difficulty prioritizing or assigning value to life events. Having a clearer sense of yourself will aid you in developing assertive skills.

We have emotional boundaries and physical boundaries. It may be easier to understand physical boundaries. Physical boundaries involve your physical person, the space your body occupies. Physical boundaries involve what you allow to happen to your physical person or self. Physical boundaries also include what you do to your body—what you eat, how you treat your body, whom you allow to touch you, how you exercise or do not exercise, etc.

Emotional boundaries define what you feel and what feelings you choose to share with others. Emotional boundaries include your inner life, a world that others do not see. Emotional boundaries include your right to your feelings; this involves knowing and honoring your feelings and being able to express your feelings. Your feelings are worthy of being honored—because they are your feelings. It is not OK to be told that your feelings "should" be different from what they are or that your feelings are "bad." Feelings are just feelings—they are not good or bad—they are the emotions that you have. Emotional boundaries speak to what you choose to give yourself to, what you value, and what you want out of life. Emotional boundaries involve your inner most feelings, recognizing your feelings, and expressing them through assertive skills. Emotional boundaries may involve listening to others and acknowledging their feelings. When you take your sister's make-up without her permission, you have broken a physical boundary. In a sense, you have trespassed into someone else's space.

If you kiss someone who doesn't want to be kissed, you have broken a physical boundary and an emotional boundary. You may not have been aware of someone else's boundaries or you may have chosen to ignore someone's boundaries. Having good boundaries may involve knowing that you have two hours of homework and not accepting phone calls between 7:00 and 9:00 pm. The issue of self interest is related to boundary issues. Really, we all focus on what it is that we want. The core of this book is about teaching ways of knowing what we want and asking for it. But we must balance what we want with a sense of what others want and how we can best respond to their wants and needs.

Being overly influenced by your peer group, especially when you do not agree with what is happening, is a good example of not following what you believe and letting your boundaries slide. Weak boundaries may involve going along with the crowd when it is not what you really want. For example: dying your hair green (and you really don't want to); trying so very hard to please your girlfriend and becoming resentful of this; giving in to others at your expense (i.e., saying "yes" when you wanted to say "no" or "maybe"); carving on yourself because you must do this to be accepted by your group; paying for everyone's lunch to make friends and not having money for the rest of the week; etc.

Boundaries involve knowing:

- Who has influence over you?
- What are your limits?
- What are you willing to do?

- What do you care about?
- For what cause or purpose are you willing to give yourself?

Examples of appropriate boundaries include:
- Deciding that it is OK for your best friend to borrow your prom dress.
- Sharing your time with a student who needs help in geometry.
- Being involved in healthy extracurricular activities.
- Not allowing other students to use or copy your school work.
- Not covering for other students if everyone says that they are at your house, but they are really over at Sam's house having a keg party.

Boundaries help us to think about what you are doing for yourself and what part of yourself you may be giving away. Boundaries help us to decide what we value and how much we value.

Physical Boundary Questions

What physical boundaries make you feel comfortable?

_____

_____

_____

_____

R U Assertive?

Do you have a space in your house that is just for you and your belongings?

Are you too demanding about your physical space?

Do you take over your room and other rooms in your house?

Techniques for Knowing Yourself

What items do you feel OK about sharing with your brother, sister, friends?

_____

_____

_____

_____

How do you treat your body . . . your most important physical boundary?

_____

_____

_____

_____

Emotional Boundary Questions

With whom, if anyone, do you want to share your deepest feelings?

_____

_____

_____

_____

R U Assertive?

What feelings do you want to have more of?

_____

_____

_____

_____

What feelings do you want to grow within you?

_____

_____

_____

_____

What feelings would you like to have less of?

_____

_____

_____

_____

Does someone tell you that your feelings don't count? or are not OK? How do you handle this?

_____

_____

_____

_____

Does someone tell you that you are not OK?

_____

_____

_____

_____

How do you handle situations when others tell you how you should feel?

_____

_____

_____

_____

After reading this book if you feel that you know yourself "less than" you desire, seek assistance from a counselor, a therapist, or a person in the helping profession to assist you in developing a stronger sense of self.

Technique #3: Drawing

For this exercise, you will need paper, crayons, or pastels—something with which to color.

Take out a piece of paper. I prefer 14" x 21" size paper, but any size will do. Draw a large circle on it. The circle can be the size of a paper plate. In my office we draw a circle around a paper plate. Once you have made the circle, then just draw. Draw whatever you want, whatever color or shape comes to you. Draw inside, outside, or on the circle; it doesn't matter. Realize that there is no art critic in the room with you. Do not judge or be critical of your drawing. Be accepting of what you draw. Draw how you feel. Do you need to draw red for anger, blue for the brother you hope disappears, pink for your best friend, etc. What color are you feeling? Remember, there are no right or wrong drawings or responses; I mentioned these colors with these emotions because they are common to that feeling state. Any color that you use is right because it is what you have chosen. Try not to think while you draw. Do not let your mind guide your drawing—just draw. Draw what you feel. Let the colors come to you. Draw without judgment. As you draw, allow yourself to release your feelings or part of you on paper. Let feelings drain out of you. If you draw once and still feel like a dam about to burst, draw again and then again. When I sit down to draw, I rarely draw one picture. I usually have to draw several drawings to get to the place where I feel relief or "ahhhh." Push yourself to work on paper. Give yourself some relief. Put your feelings on paper—in color. If there is someone with whom you are upset and unhappy, you may have lots of pent up feelings about that person—feelings that need to go somewhere. Perhaps you are furious with your brother. If you have these feelings and in your anger you hit your brother or break his toys, etc. you will get in trouble. Perhaps what you feel is that you will get relief by smashing or tearing up his toys or his homework. You will do something "to get even" with him—but this is not true. In truth, you can not "get even" with anyone. The most that you can do is to help yourself by "owning" what you truly feel. Own you emotions, whether they are love, hate, happiness, disgust, distrust, despise, etc. Give yourself permission to feel that feeling and release it, give voice to the feeling by putting it down on paper, by giving it color. Acknowledge and respect feelings but do not let them control you. To honor a feeling is to allow yourself to know that the feeling is present; to honor your feelings does not mean that you act on your feelings.

Honoring a feeling means that you are "in touch" with what is going on inside you, your feelings or emotional self. You allow a feeling or an emotional self to be known, to be. This is not as easy as it may appear. You may have been brought up in a house

Techniques for Knowing Yourself

where you are a "coward" or a "baby" if you cry. Then, you may feel that it is not OK to have feelings of vulnerability or to cry. Try to give yourself permission to just acknowledge what you are feeling; again, try not to judge your feelings.

If you draw, you will give yourself relief. This may not be a "relief" that you are used to, but it is the kind of relief where if you are carrying three suitcases, you feel lighter because you get to put two suitcases down.

Also, never judge what you draw and don't feel that it must in any way represent or look like your feelings. That is, if you are angry and you draw daisies—that is OK; just be with what you create in color on paper. Moreover, I encourage all of my clients to keep their drawings private. Their drawings may reflect their most intimate self, so guard whom you allow to see your drawings.

To express your feelings in color, in writing, etc. does not mean that the emotion will grow stronger in you. I have had clients who were fearful and worried about drawing their anger because they thought that to acknowledge their feelings would be to give the feelings strength or power. They felt that "bad" feelings would grow in them, even "take them over." This is not true. To acknowledge the feeling is to give acceptance to yourself, to be fully human, to have emotional depth. To "own" a feeling is to give strength or power to yourself. The lesson is to recognize a feeling, honor a feeling, and then to let go of the feeling, to release the feeling. Clients also tell me that they feel guilty if they have harsh feelings toward others and they draw and put those feelings on paper. Again, the concept is to allow the feelings, express the feelings in color, and then let go of the feelings. Can you imagine that feelings are bubbles inside of you and that as you draw, you "release" some of the bubbles and let them drift away? You have the feeling and then you let go of the feeling. If you keep negative emotions in you, they will begin to color how you feel, affecting your mind and your health. But if you give yourself permission to just feel what you are feeling and then release the feeling, you are acknowledging or empowering yourself. You honor yourself by being truthful to yourself. You are giving yourself strength because you are not alienating your feelings from yourself. Also, it may take many exercises of drawing to begin to feel that you are acknowledging and then letting go of an issue or a thought. Be patient with yourself and your drawings.

It is sometimes difficult to understand that if we do not acknowledge "negative" emotions such as pain, anger, disgust, etc. as well as what we think of as more positive emotions—such as love, peace, joy, etc., we are in some way putting a lid, a lock so to speak, on the joy and happiness that we can experience. You cannot escape or cut out one emotion (anger) and have only positive emotions (peace). If you lie to yourself and tell yourselves that you do not have negative emotions, you take something away from yourself.

If you try to distance yourself from hate and anger and other "negative" emotions, it is as if you are cutting off your hand or your arm. These emotions are also a part of you. They help to make you who you are; they make you whole. You are less complete when you distance yourself from emotions that you have come to think of as negative. One of the issues becomes learning to trust yourself. The words in this book can provide guidance, but only you can choose which path you will take when it comes to your feelings. Be patient with yourself as you learn to feel different feelings. Trust in self does not happen immediately; it is a process of growing stronger in knowing yourself, believing in yourself, and putting your thoughts and feelings into action.

Now, how to deal with those situations where you have parents who believe that it is evil or wrong to have what we call "negative" emotions? Your parents may be afraid of some of their own feelings; so, they have trouble acknowledging their feelings, and may not want to honor in you the feelings that they discount in themselves. One way of dealing with this situation is to try to trust yourself. Believe that you are on the right path and that it is more healing to be in touch with your feelings and the truth than to distance yourself from your emotions. You "shrink" yourself when you keep your true feelings from yourself—even if they are feelings of contempt, anger, hostility, etc.

Techniques for Knowing Yourself

If you live in a household where you are encouraged to deny certain feelings, ask your parents to read this book; maybe you can help them to understand that your intent in learning assertive skills and by acknowledging your "negative" feelings is not to be disrespectful. Your intent is to know yourself, to grow stronger as a person, and to learn to speak up for yourself.

In my practice as a therapist a significant aspect of psychological work is to help clients reclaim their true feelings. Joan Borysenko points out in her book *Guilt is the Teacher, Love is the Lesson* (1990) that we grow up trying to please others and as a result we stuff those parts of ourselves that are not "pretty" into an invisible bag that we drag beside us day in and day out. What is in the bag? The bag contains the parts of ourselves we deny. The feelings that we deny can be called shadow selves. The shadow involves those aspects of ourselves which are unknown to us. The shadow consists of all the "parts" of us that we were told were not "okay." Your shadow self or your unknown self can also contain good or positive attributes or it may be parts of yourself that carry shame and feelings of unworthiness. I have a lady friend who owns several businesses and I asked her how she is able to do this successfully without being overly stressed. She does not have a large staff or employees; however, she carries on the work of multiple persons with ease and grace. How does she accomplish this? She reports that she has less "suitcases" than the rest of us because she deals with her feelings and emotions on a regular basis. That is to say, she has less baggage or shadow parts than the rest of us. She has dealt with her painful past. Part of her life work is to persevere in emptying the bags and suitcases that fill up the shadow and to keep moving.

To summarize, give yourself permission to be OK with whatever you draw on paper. Practice giving yourself permission to be OK with yourself. Practice drawing a circle and coloring for relief and for fun.

Technique #4: Writing Sprints

Another step in getting to know yourself and in helping to develop your assertive skills is to practice Writing Sprints. Writing Sprints involve writing out the remainder of a sentence stem. A sentence stem is a few words that begin a writing exercise. Writing sprints involve writing out a few words that start a sentence or a thought and then very quickly writing out all that you think and feel.

When completing a writing sprint, it is important to write fast and furious for three to five minutes based on your tolerance for this exercise. This writing exercise has nothing to do with your high school English class. The purpose of writing sprints is to write with no thought of errors, punctuation, content, spelling, etc. The idea is to rapidly put your thoughts down on paper. Also, this must be a private exercise. If you think or know that someone is going to read what you wrote, you may not write your true feelings or thoughts. You may not get in touch with your true feelings and what you write may be contaminated or restricted. If your written words reflect what others think of you, then you may not be true to yourself, to your true emotions.

These are examples of sentence stems:

Today I feel . . .

I wish my boyfriend would . . .

When Mom talks to me like that . . .

Today at school I felt . . .

When my sister . . .

I am really angry about . . .

If only I could . . .

Now, practice a writing sprint . . . write fast and furious for 3 or 5 minutes. If you go off course from your original topic, don't worry, just write. Read what you wrote, keep it in a safe place, or

Techniques for Knowing Yourself

tear it up. You may want to keep a journal of your writing sprints. Remember, the most important idea is to write quickly, put a time frame on your writing exercises, and, most importantly, keep it private. Perhaps your parents may be willing to purchase a paper shredder if you are worried about privacy. That way you can destroy your writings when you have completed them.

> *A student who I worked with in private practice had a very impulsive temper. He often became angry with students and would sometimes hit other students. One day at school he became angry with a classmate. Instead of hitting the student, he sat down and wrote a writing sprint about the student and his anger toward him. Then, he put his writing sprint in the trash can in his classroom. The teacher thought that the paper in the trash can was a school work assignment, picked it out of the trash can, and read it. The teacher was very troubled by what the student wrote and called the student's parents. The parents called me and I then called the teacher and explained what had happened. The teacher then realized that the student had contained his anger by not hitting the other student. This was significant improvement for my client; in the past he might have hit another student and been suspended. Thus, the teacher was able to appreciate the student's actions and his ability to gain control over his actions and his temper. Also, the student learned a valuable lesson about keeping his writing sprints private.*

At different times use these stems to produce a writing sprint:

I am unhappy about...

I would like to fix...

Last night when James gave directions...

After the football game I...

Dad makes me feel...

I am frustrated because...

I frequently use writing sprints to deal with family members and home issues. It is not unusual for me to write about flushing one of my children down the toilet. I adore this child and I waited many long years for him to come; yet, there are many days when I feel that if I could stuff all of his 6'3" frame in the toilet, I would gladly do so. It doesn't mean that I don't love him and he isn't a joy, because he is. But as he moves through teenage years, he brings me pain and grief as well as joy and fulfillment. Many times, I feel that I have failed him as a mother. I write about that, too. And I also write about my lack of control in his life, as he grows into a man.

I feel safe writing sprints about family members because they are considered "sacred space" in our house. They are a good example of a boundary issue. If my writing sprints are left out, family members know that they are not to read them—that they are mom's heart thoughts, frustrations, hopes, etc. on paper. Also, family members know to return them to me—because I have misplaced something important.

Technique #5: Breathing

Breath is a very important key to life. After thirty years of work, I have yet to meet a teenager who can breathe right—even the well-developed athletes that I see do not know the correct procedures for breathing. Learning how to breathe correctly will help you learn to get in touch with yourself and your emotions, which in turn will help you learn to know yourself and speak up for yourself.

There are many different approaches that can be used in learning how to breathe more deeply and more fully. I think that Dr. Andrew Weil's approach to breath work, *Breathing the Master Key to Self-Healing* (1999), has both balance and practicality. This is the process that I teach my clients, and it is similar to Dr. Weil's techniques:

Techniques for Knowing Yourself

1. Find a place where you will not be distracted. You may want to include music in this exercise, especially if the music has a calming effect.
2. Sit up straight and tall with an erect spine—you may need to put a pillow behind your back.
3. Put your hands on your stomach—you will learn to feel your stomach rise and fall as you breathe. This is called "stomach breathing." Your stomach should extend as you breathe. See the picture on the next page for visual assistance.
4. As you learn to breathe, practice inhaling with your nose and exhaling with your mouth. Keep your hand on your stomach, making sure that it rises and falls. You may want to purse your lips to control your exhalation.
5. Exhale to begin this exercise and then begin the inhalation process. With each inhalation, pull the breath down into your stomach (this is actually the lower section of your lungs, but you need to feel it in the rise and fall of your stomach) and then slowly fill up your chest as you count to five.
6. Hold that breath for five counts.
7. Exhale that breath to a count of five or six slowly releasing the air from your body. The breath should leave from your stomach **first** and you should feel your stomach flatten as you let the air deflate out of your chest.
8. Continue with this pattern for ten minutes and then work up to fifteen minutes.
9. Try to do your breath work at a regular pace.

INHALE   EXHALE

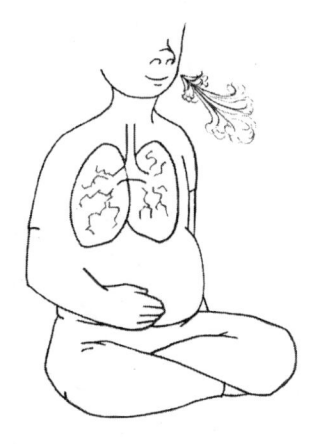

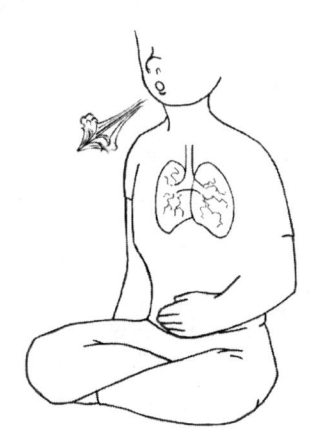

To summarize how to breathe: Inhale to a count of five, hold to a count of five, exhale to a count of five or six. Inhale through your nose and exhale out of your mouth. Focus on your breath. Thoughts will come and go; gently acknowledge them, and return your focus to your breath. Try to practice breathing correctly 5 or 10 minutes a day. Over time you can build up the count of breaths as well as the amount of time that you are practicing.

This simple art of learning how to breathe can help you learn to have better control over the stressors in your life. Also, as you "quiet your mind" by focusing on your breath and by not being so distracted by the outside world i.e., TV, video games, computers, homework, friends, etc., you will eventually come to know yourself better. You will feel that you have more control over yourself.

Technique #6: Relaxation Exercises

Relaxation exercises are another way of taking care of yourself, knowing more about yourself, and growing stronger. In today's society, you can become distant from yourself and not realize how your body feels and how that affects your feelings. I believe that our feelings are intertwined with our physical being and cannot be separated. Perhaps science is not at a place where this can be proven—but the old adage that she felt "sick to her stomach" after she learned that she failed her math course probably has merit. This is a good example of how your feelings affect your physical body.

Sometimes we internalize (i.e., take in) our emotional states. This means that your feelings become part of you. You may "stuff" your feelings and emotions inside of your body. Just as my brown eyes and brown hair are a recognizable part of me, your feelings, though unseen and often unrecognizable, are a strong part of you. When you do not acknowledge your feelings or "own them" **they do not go away**. Not known doesn't mean not present. Because your feelings touch the physical part of your being, when you learn relaxation techniques you will be getting in touch with your body and with your feelings and emotions. One of the best relaxation techniques consists of tightening and relaxing your muscles. We're going to go through an exercise of tensing and relaxing muscles. This may leave you feeling more relaxed and in touch with yourself.

Read these exercises first and then practice.

1. Close your eyes. Get in touch with your breath. Are you breathing quickly or slowly? Don't try to change your breath, just pay attention to how you are breathing.

2. Bring your attention to your right hand and pretend that you have a small ball in your right hand and squeeze it as tightly as you can, trying to press all of the air out of it. Use your muscles; do not push your nails into the palm of your hand. Press on the imaginary ball, then release. Complete this exercise three times with each hand. Notice the difference in your hands and arms when you are pressing hard into the pretend ball. How do you feel when your muscles are tight and tense? How do you feel when your muscles are relaxed? Begin to notice the difference in feeling relaxed in your body and in feeling tense.

3. Try to touch your shoulders to your ears and hold for five seconds. Complete this exercise three times.

4. Scrunch your face up like you just drank something sour and then relax. Do this three times.

5. Hold your stomach in tightly, and try to press your stomach to your backbone. Go slowly. Then relax. Do this three times

6. Make your thighs hard and then relax. Do this three times.

7. Put your feet flat on the floor and push deeply into the floor, as if you are descending to another floor below this one. Then relax. Do this exercise three times.

Take a deep breath in and relax. Feel the tension draining out of your muscles and into the floor, out of the room, and to other spaces. Feel your body become slightly warmer as you relax.

Try to practice these exercises three or four times a week. The more you practice, the better you will become at relaxing. The more you practice, the more you can rely on these exercises to help you in stressful situations. You can't practice for a few weeks and expect to put your body into a state of relaxation. However, if you practice on a regular basis, these exercises may be helpful in calming yourself before your math test, in asking that special girl out on a date, in bringing calm to your body before that important basketball game, etc. Some of my clients practice these exercises before they go to sleep at night. The exercises help them relax into sleep and provide a good boundary between the day's activities and transitioning to the night and to sleep.

Chapter 4
Self-Knowledge Leads to Self-Advocacy

In this chapter you will take the skills that you have learned in previous chapters and begin to use them so that you can become your best advocate or cheerleader. You will learn strategies that will deepen your knowledge of yourself, what you truly feel, and how you can communicate more fully with others. You will develop more skills for listening to yourself and your feelings. You may find that you have conflict between your head and your heart when you are making decisions; you will explore ways to resolve this conflict and make decisions using your assertive skills.

What is self-advocacy? Self-advocacy is a way of taking care of yourself. To be a self-advocate means to know yourself and to speak up for yourself. Why does self-advocacy matter? To be a self-advocate is powerful because you are in charge of yourself. Your parents are your first advocates and, hopefully, they have modeled for you how to speak up for yourself and how to take care of yourself. However, there may never be another person as good as you at taking care of yourself. Who is in the best position to take care of you? To know you? To speak up for you? **You are.** Your job is to be **your best advocate**. No one else will ever be in as good a position as you are to know what is in your mind and what is in your heart. You must learn to vocalize your feelings for yourself. Your life, your happiness, and your fulfillment may depend on how you deal with these issues.

To know yourself means to be clear about who you are, what you want, and what you must do to reach your goals.

Who are you when you are alone? Do you realize that you may be different with each group with which you associate (i.e., your family, friends, team members, church friends, etc.)? When your friends are not available, when you are just by yourself—this is one aspect of you. When you are with your friends, how do you act? This may be another aspect of you. Who do you represent to your friends? Whose son or daughter are you? How do you feel about who you are? These questions speak to responses/answers regarding who you are. You are actually a blend of many aspects that represent you. As you grow older, and as you develop more knowledge about who you are, you will be able to develop better assertive skills.

It is important to recognize that there are big and small ways of taking care of yourself. A less important way of taking care of yourself may be by asking your brother to move his clothes, toys, etc. off of your bed so that you can go to sleep. Stating what you need/want can be as simple as that. Or, to be an advocate can be much more demanding. A more demanding situation might involve telling another student that you do not feel OK helping him to cheat on an algebra test, not joining your friends at a drinking party, or telling your father who was a baseball pro that you want to play the piano, and not play baseball.

When your teacher talks fast during the class lecture, you can't keep up. Who knows this? Your best friend, Jacob? Your girlfriend, Samantha? Your football teammate, Chris? No. Only you are aware of this because only you have this knowledge. No one knows as well as you what your needs are, what your desires are, and what you want. This book is about helping you get in touch with those needs and expressing them in the right manner. In the preceding example there are different scenarios that could have taken place. The student could have been assertive by going

Self-knowledge Leads to Self-advocacy

to the teacher and stating, "I'm having trouble taking notes as you speak. What else can you offer for help? Can you give me a written copy of your notes or can I have a student take notes for me (i.e., a student note taker)?"

Another example of dealing with this school situation that would not be wise would be verbal put downs of the teacher. This may involve making remarks like, "I hate Mrs. Jones. She yaps so fast that no one in class can keep up with her. I wish she'd retire or get fired." Statements such as these do not involve assertive skills, and will not help you meet your needs.

Self-advocacy involves using assertive skills. Self-advocacy also involves self-knowledge and self-care taking.

Self-advocacy involves the use of assertive skills by knowing what you need, stating the need clearly, and following through so that the need can be met. This process, of using assertive skills, is not as easy as it may appear to be. How can you become a better self-advocate? We'll explore several methods beginning with developing a better awareness of your feelings. Let's practice by looking at several areas of your life and exploring how you feel.

Practice Exercises

How do you feel about school? What do you like about school? If you had a magic wand, what would you change about school?

_____

_____

_____

_____

_____

R U Assertive?

How do you feel about your best friend? How long has this person been your friend? How would you like to change the relationship? What makes you comfortable in this relationship?

_____
_____
_____
_____
_____
_____
_____

Write about how your family makes you feel. What do you like/dislike about your parents? How do you feel about your brother(s) or sister(s)? How would you like for things to stay the same at your house? How would you like for things to change?

_____
_____
_____
_____
_____
_____
_____
_____

Self-knowledge Leads to Self-advocacy

How do you feel right now? What makes you feel good about yourself? Your life? What changes would you like to make?

_____

_____

_____

_____

_____

_____

_____

_____

Examine the responses. You may have written different responses to the same question. Your answers may change day to day or week to week. That's OK. Which statements are closest to what you truly feel? One way to get in touch with this is to notice what makes you feel better in your stomach. I am referring to the stomach because the stomach is often the place where emotions are present in your physical body. Your stomach may be your "feeling" place. When you are upset and someone has treated you badly, you may feel "sick to your stomach." This may reflect that some of your feelings have settled into that place in your body and are causing some upset.

Back to your responses—if none of the responses "feels right," write out other statements regarding how you feel. I know that these exercises take time; however, as we grow older, it may become more difficult to find your true feelings and to express them. Your feelings may be cluttered by your desire to please others and to please your parents, as well as trying to please siblings, boyfriends, girlfriends, teachers, coaches, etc. In your effort to please others, you may have lost sight of your true self and what you think and feel. Or, there may also be situations when you are told that your feelings do not count, when someone else's will or desire is greater than or more important than "your feelings." In this situation your feelings may have become blocked or stuffed because they are overshadowed by another person's will or desires.

Are you a people pleaser? Do you want to make everyone happy? Do you want to keep the peace? Do you please others—at an expense to yourself? Do you deny what you want and feel in order to please someone else? How does this make you feel? Does it make you "numb" or less able to locate or be with your feelings? What would it take for you to state what you truly want? or need? If your boyfriend keeps asking you to have sex with him—and you are uncomfortable with this, do you feel like you have to give in order to keep him in your life?

Sometimes it's difficult to identify your true feelings because you are too self-focused. The opposite of wanting to please others is being self-focused. This may involve being so wrapped up in yourself that you are overly focused on yourself and can't sort out a clear definition of what you feel at the moment. Although you may be focused on yourself you may have trouble identifying what you feel. It is possible to be very focused on yourself *and* not be in touch with your true feelings.

At the core of all of us is the issue of worth. What are we worth? Physically, the sum total of a person's body may not be worth much—perhaps a few dollars—but the truth is that you are beyond value. You have great worth. Why do you not act like you are a person who is worthy of being treated well? Perhaps, sometime in growing up you got the message that "I am not OK . . . you are OK, but I am not." It may take years for this negative message to develop—so this message can not be quickly overcome. The important lesson here is that students, parents, teachers, etc. often treat you how you **feel** you deserve to be treated. If you care for yourself and believe in yourself, you will convey this message to others. But, if you have low self-esteem and feel that you are a failure, have failed in many ways, or do not feel that you "make

Self-knowledge Leads to Self-advocacy

the mark," you will give others the **message that they can treat you however they please**. This is not OK. If this is a significant problem, a good idea is to find a counselor or a therapist who can help you chip away at your feelings of lack of self-worth and help you develop a stronger you.

Do not let negative feelings about yourself allow you to engage in acts that will put you or your health at risk or even destroy you.

Because we may be "out of touch" with our true feelings and desires I am including a feeling checklist to help you identify your feelings.

Positive Feelings	Negative Feelings	Uncertain Feelings
Happy	Unhappy	Mystified
Content	Sad	Frustrated
Good	Mad	Listless
Pleased	Upset	Questioning
Joyful	Bummed Out	Dicey
Satisfied	Trashed Out	Concerned
Jubilant	Sick	Unsure
Awesome	Dissed	Anxious
Exuberance	Troubled	Sketchy
Encouraged	Trashed	Bewildered
Confident	Accused	Confused
Excited	Worried	Speechless
Respected	Worthless	Uneasy
Grateful	Put down	Nervous
Comfortable	Inadequate	Jittery

Positive Feelings	Negative Feelings	Uncertain Feelings
Glad	Hopeless	Wishy-washy
Enjoyed	Embarrassed	Pressured
Fulfilled	Defeated	Preoccupied
Hopeful	Pissed	Hesitant
Proud	Harassed	Tentative
Alive	Desperate	Doubtful
Accepted	Dreadful	Apprehensive
Certain	Helpless	Unsettled
Assured	Hurt	Uncomfortable

It may be important to temporarily memorize these words because stating how you feel, "owning" your feelings, may not naturally occur. Memorizing these feelings will help you own your feelings and express yourself. If you aren't clear about your internal state, how can others be clear? How can your friends "read" you correctly if you don't know what you are feeling?

At first it may be confusing to learn who you are, what you want, to speak up for yourself, to claim your assertive right, and at the same time to be respectful to adults and authority figures.

Anything new can be challenging. Change may be hard. Knowing that you are worthy and speaking up for yourself may not be easy. But as you practice, it gets easier, and you gain confidence and a greater sense of who you are.

There is a difference between knowing who you are and what you want and being under the supervision of "higher authorities" such as your parents, teachers, police, etc. I tell my clients, "This is not a Cinderella world." What does that mean? You can't magically make things happen. You can't become assertive just by wanting to be more of a spokesperson for yourself. You need to work. In this case it means that there is not an "assertive

Self-knowledge Leads to Self-advocacy

wand" that will magically bring your wants, needs, or desires to you. Getting to know yourself and what you feel about yourself may not be an easy task. Getting in touch with your true feelings and emotions doesn't give you a right to be demanding, forceful, or unreasonable. It does give you a right to be honored as an individual, to be worthy of having a voice, and of being "heard." It gives you a right to be in touch with your feelings and state them. This does not mean your every wish will be granted. It does mean that you will have a better chance of getting what you want, because as you grow stronger in yourself you will take care of yourself by giving a voice to your wants and needs. Are your parents psychic? No. Are your teachers psychic? No. Can people read your mind? No. Even your best friend cannot read your mind and often does not know what is in your heart. I love the cartoon that shows a very frustrated and unhappy wife on the golf course with her husband on her birthday and the caption shows the husband saying: "You told me to plan something that would be enjoyable." This did not mean that the wife wanted to spend her birthday playing 18 holes of golf. But she did not speak up; she was not clear about her wishes and desires. The results reflect her lack of assertiveness—which ended up in a birthday that involved 18 holes of golf for this wife.

How much better her birthday would have been if she had clearly spoken up about her true birthday wishes. It could have gone something like this: "Honey, my first choices would be 1) a day of shopping at the mall, 2) a visit to see Aunt Mary, or 3) time in the morning with my sister and then time in the afternoon with you and the kids at the park."

Do you hear any mention of golf in the preceding suggestions? No. Rather than feel confused, frustrated, and disappointed, speak up for yourself. Get quiet within yourself and figure out what you truly want to happen. Ask yourself, "What would be my ideal birthday or anniversary? What would I like to see happen? What would need to happen for me to enjoy this situation? Who do I need to say? How can I get this message to the right people? With school activities you might ask, "How do I want the student council meeting to be run?" You may need to ask who you want to involve in situations for them to be successful. When you identify what you want, there are no guarantees that you will succeed. However, you are less likely to meet your goals and plans if you are not clear with yourself and others about what you want.

Imagine this: Perhaps a girl wants to spend Saturday night at the movies and her boyfriend wants to go bowling. He asks her what she wants to do and she says, "Whatever you want to do." She really did care, but she did not express her true feelings. At the bowling alley she is miserable and ends up fighting with her boyfriend. How could this have been avoided? Even if he had not asked about the evening, it would have been wise for her to state what she wanted to happen . . . not what she **thought** would please someone else. In this case, the girl was not true to herself, and she suffered from "pleaser" syndrome. She felt that if she just did whatever her boyfriend wanted to do, all would be well. Her misery boiled up inside of her and it spilled over into an argument with her boyfriend.

Assertive communication would have helped this situation. Even if the boy and girl had first negotiated how they would spend one Saturday night doing an activity that he liked (i.e., bowling) and the next Saturday night doing an activity that she may have chosen (i.e., going to the movies), the result would have been more positive. Perhaps she would have been less angry with her boyfriend on Saturday night if she knew that the next weekend she would have an activity of her choice. This might have made her Saturday night bowling more bearable.

Logical Self and Feeling Self

As you come to know more about yourself, you learn that there is a logical self (your brain self or thinking self) and a feeling self (your heart self).

What is the difference between our head and our heart? How do these issues fit in with assertive skills?

The head is the logical part of our being. It is the thinking self.

Self-knowledge Leads to Self-advocacy

The heart is our feeling self. More often than not the heart is the keeper of our feelings and our emotions.

During elementary school years, there may be more balance between your head and your heart. You think, you feel, and you respond from one place that is within you. During teenage years you may feel more of a divide in yourself—a split between your head and your heart. You may feel one way about a situation, but think an opposite way about what is going on. You may be struggling to find out who you truly are and you may "try on" many identities. It is during these years that you may tend to be ruled by your heart, especially teenage girls. That is, your heart may govern your actions. You may "carry your heart on your sleeve" and you may let your feelings be the engine that drives the train.

During these years there is wisdom in trying to see situations with both your head and your heart, because you may be "out of balance."

It is important to know who you are and what you want. If you do not know yourself, you cannot be assertive, and cannot speak up for yourself. You may be like a small boat on the ocean, instead of a large ship. When a good storm comes along, the small boat is at risk for being tossed and turned by the sea—and turned into a pile of wood—no longer a worthy seagoing boat. In order to balance these issues, girls in particular, may benefit from giving more attention to their heads than their hearts.

Work with **cause** and **effect** can help balance out your feelings between your head and your heart. What is cause and effect and why is it so important? Cause and effect means that for every action there is a consequence, a result.

For example, if I do this what will happen? What will be the result of my actions? How will this affect me? my family? As a therapist I refer to this process as "connecting the dots." Do you remember when you were a little person (5 or 6 years old) and you had a drawing with either numbers or letters of the alphabet that were scattered all over the page? When you connected the dots with the numbers or the letters, a shape emerged. The image became clear when all of the dots were connected. I refer to cause and effect as "connecting the dots" because you need to see that each action of yours will lead to a result, a consequence. For example, if someone breaks a vase in a store, someone must pay for it. The action is the breaking of the vase, and the consequence is parting with money. Cause and effect is always operating in a known and in an unknown (unseen) way. To operate in an "unseen" way means that you may not see or feel the immediate effect of your actions, but your actions have created a consequence, a result, whether you know it or not. Your words cause happiness, pain, hope, suffering, etc. Your actions touch both your life and the lives of others.

Using cause and effect thinking ask yourself these questions:

- What am I doing that is going to help me? or hurt me?
- To what will my actions lead? How will my actions affect those that I love?
- How will my actions effect others? With these questions in the back of your mind you can direct your actions in a logical, thinking way, and balance your thinking self (head) and your feeling self (heart).

Practice Exercises

List three situations where you were ruled by your head.

_____

_____

_____

_____

_____

_____

Self-knowledge Leads to Self-advocacy

List three situations where you were ruled by your heart.

List three situations where you were ruled by your head and your heart.

R U Assertive?

When we don't use our heart and our head to make decisions, sometimes we make decisions very quickly—without thinking. Sometimes we are impulsive and are driven by what we want at the moment. We can reduce our impulsivity by stopping and thinking and using cause and effect strategies. Then you need to use your assertive skills to clearly express what you want or need. There are many exercises that may be useful in helping you to know yourself at a deeper level. The following are exercises you may wish to use as you grow clearer about yourself and your desires while you are learning to express yourself.

Practice Exercises

Draw three symbols that represent you.

Self-knowledge Leads to Self-advocacy

What about the symbols makes you think of yourself? Draw a symbol that represents you in six months.

Draw a symbol that represents you in one year.

R U Assertive?

Draw a symbol that represents you in five years.

Additional questions that will give you insight into who you are:
- What are your goals?
- How would you like to change in the next six months?
- How would you like to see yourself in one year?
- What would you like to do when you grow up?
- How would you want to be when you grow up?

Care for Self

Care for self matters. If you haven't gotten enough sleep lately, if you're eating a lot of junk food, if your girlfriend just broke up with you, or if you're having hormone issues, it may be more challenging to be assertive. Know this and be patient with yourself. Practice physical and emotional self-care. To practice physical self-care means to eat right, get enough sleep, and exercise. To take care of your emotional self means to have some fun, to be in touch with your emotions, and to express them.

Self-care also involves being an advocate for yourself and using assertive skills. As much as possible, practice assertive skills daily—the more you practice the better you will be at identifying what you want, stating what you want, and identifying your emotional concerns. Self-knowledge involves a deeper knowledge of who you are and what you want. Answer these questions about yourself:

Practice Exercises
Self-Knowledge Questions:
What do you like about yourself?

What would you like to change?

What steps are necessary for change?

R U Assertive?

What are some of your goals?

___

How can you meet those goals?

___

What behaviors that are unkind are you willing to tolerate from your "friends?" Do they make unkind remarks about you? Why do you stay connected to people who treat you badly?

___

If you feel you need more assistance than this book can provide, seek professional help through your school guidance counselor, a helping teacher, or a therapist.

Chapter 5
Learning Disabilities, Dyslexia, AD/HD, and NLD
Why are they Important Factors in Learning Assertive Skills?

The previous chapters have focused on learning about your feelings, developing assertive skills, and learning techniques for expressing your wants and needs in an appropriate manner. You will continue to focus on those skills in this chapter, but you will also read about learning differences and attention problems. This chapter is included in this book because learning differences and attention problems have potential to lessen or even to destroy your ability to express yourself. If you learn differently or if you are inattentive, distractible, or impulsive, there is a far greater chance that you will be misunderstood by your peer group, by the adults in your life, by family members, etc. One way to combat the challenges that come with learning and attention problems is for you to be more deeply in touch with your needs and to effectively use assertive skills. Students who learn differently or who have attention deficits may have a greater need for assertive skills. This is because they are more likely to miss cues, to be distracted (internally and externally), and to be impulsive. This chapter will provide a brief overview of students who learn differently and/or who have attentional concerns. Addressing assertive skills in light of these learning or attentional differences will also be discussed.

Students who have AD/HD or learning problems are provided assistance through three federal laws. These laws include the Individuals with Disabilities Education Improvement Act (Public Law No: 108-446), Section 504 of the Rehabilitation Act of 1973, and the American with Disabilities Act of 1990. Under IDEA students are eligible for an evaluation to assess for learning disabilities and for a free and appropriate education. The evaluation is very important in defining how you learn best, and if you are exhibiting learning or attentional problems. Also, it is common for students who have AD/HD to have learning problems and for students who learn differently to have symptoms of AD/HD. It is important to distinguish these issues through a comprehensive evaluation. You can contact your local school district office, the State Department of Education, or the Department of Education for complete information regarding these laws and how to access services.

Attention-Deficit/Hyperactivity Disorder

Attention-Deficit/Hyperactivity Disorder (AD/HD) is a neurological (brain) condition that can be exhibited by significant difficulty in attention, impulsivity, and distractibility. It can also involve overactivity. The definition and diagnosis of AD/HD comes from *The Diagnostic and Statistical Manual of Mental Disorders*, Fourth Edition TR (2000). In this book I will make reference to all forms of attention deficit as AD/HD; however, there are three subtypes of AD/HD. They include the following:

- predominantly inattentive
- predominantly hyperactive and impulsive
- combined type which includes inattentive, hyperactive, and impulsive

To have AD/HD a student should exhibit the symptoms by age seven; however, many students are not identified as having AD/HD until the symptoms significantly interfere with their academic skills. Moreover, the symptoms for each subtype must be more frequent and severe than a typical student would exhibit. That is, all of us may exhibit some of these symptoms from time to time, but if a student has AD/HD, these symptoms represent a pattern that will not go away. In order to be identified as having AD/HD the symptoms must be present in two or more settings (i.e., school, work, or home) and the symptoms must have a negative impact on social, school, or work skills.

The following is a list of the symptoms of inattention. A student should exhibit at least six of these symptoms for a diagnosis of predominantly inattentive type AD/HD:

Inattention:

- failure to give close attention to details and makes careless errors
- has difficulty keeping attention going
- does not seem to listen when spoken to directly
- does not follow through on instructions and fails to complete school work, chores, or duties
- has difficulty organizing tasks and activities
- avoids, dislikes, or is resistant to engage in tasks that require concentration (i.e. schoolwork or homework)
- loses items necessary for tasks or activities (i.e. toys, books, assignments, tools, etc.)
- is easily distracted (may be distracted by auditory, visual, or tactile stimuli)
- is forgetful in daily activities (i.e. forgets to brush teeth or hair, may not keep adequate hygiene, etc.)

Six or more of the following symptoms of hyperactivity (i.e., overactivity) and impulsivity must be present for a student to exhibit predominantly hyperactive-impulsive type:

Hyperactivity:

- fidgets with hands or feet or squirms in seat
- has difficulty remaining seated in the classroom or in other situations in which remaining seated is required
- ran about or climbed excessively as a child
- has difficulty playing or engaging in leisure activities quietly
- as a child was often "on the go" or acted as if he was "driven by a motor"
- talks excessively

Impulsivity:

- blurts out answers before questions are complete
- has difficulty waiting or taking turns
- interrupts or intrudes on others in conversations or games

It is important to note that no two AD/HD students are alike. Each AD/HD student will manifest the previous symptoms in different ways, in different settings, and to different degrees.

Many AD/HD students that I have worked with are often more sensitive to what is going on in their environment than are their peers. AD/HD students can be very sensitive to their feelings and to the feelings of others. However, they may lack both the coping skills and the communication skills that are necessary for expressing their feelings in an appropriate manner. Like all of us, there are times when an AD/HD student is out of touch with his true feelings. However, there are occasions when an AD/HD student's ability to verbally state his feelings may not be adequate.

AD/HD students often miss cues in relating to others in their environment. Because they may have missed a cue, they may be confused about what is going on because their actions may seem out of place or not connected to what is happening. Other students may be talking about their plans for Friday night, and an AD/HD student—who may be impulsive and inattentive—and may not have plans for Friday night, may talk about how his favorite baseball team played last night. Other students respond by looking at the student with a look that says, "What planet are you on?" The AD/HD student may respond with some anger or irritation at not being accepted or understood. It is possible that the AD/HD student missed the cues in the conversation, and responded "out of context." This becomes a negative feedback loop. See drawing.

What are you doing Friday night?

Going to the ball game with Sarah.

Wonder where I left my math homework?

Do you have plans after the game?

ADHD Student

Let's go to Rick's house after the ball game.

Executive Skills

Executive Skills are a management or a governing system that is located in the front part of the brain. This biological system serves as a "Gatekeeper." A Gatekeeper is one who watches over things, the one who is in charge of what happens. For example, a sheep herder can be thought of as a Gatekeeper. The sheep herder (Gatekeeper) guides the sheep in knowing what pasture to go to for food, where to get water, how to seek shelter from a storm, etc. The sheep are dependent on the sheep herder (Gatekeeper) for food, for knowing how to live, etc. The Gatekeeper in your brain serves a similar function: it is a manager. It is the part of you that helps you monitor or watch your behavior.

Executive skills are associated with **cause** and **effect**. These are the tools that help you "put on the brakes" when you are invited to a keg party on Saturday night. Your Gatekeeper should automatically inform you to stop and listen to what you have been asked to do, to consider the choices that you have before you, and to consider the consequences of your actions or your behavior. When the Gatekeeper is working well, you realize that a keg party will lead to trouble for several reasons. The issues involve underage drinking, driving, impulsive acts, etc. You may also be lying to your parents if you told them that you would be at the movies, but you are really at a keg party. If you have AD/HD, executive skills may not be working well for you. Your Gatekeeper may not be adequately watching over your decision making processes or your actions. This biological tool does not always work at an adequate level in an AD/HD student. It is important for an AD/HD student to develop an awareness of what skills work well and which skills may be lacking. For example, an AD/HD student may make decisions impulsively, without enough thought. These decisions can appear to be simple, but they may cause significant problems once the consequences of the decisions have been realized. Once a student develops an awareness of these issues, developing coping strategies for these issues is very important.

This is where assertive skills can be a powerful tool for an

AD/HD student. Perhaps one of the strongest assertive skills that an AD/HD student can have is to ask questions. I don't mean inappropriately blurting out questions that will clear up what is happening. An AD/HD student does not want to commit a social-verbal blunder. For example, rather than jump into the conversation, **stop** and **listen:** What are the other students talking about? Is there a pattern in this conversation? Is everyone talking about the same thing? Are there different conversations going on? Then, stop and think about these questions regarding your input in the conversation: What can I contribute? Is it a good time to be silent, or to ask questions? How can I make a statement that fits in with the conversation?

You do not have to overwhelm your mind by asking yourself all of these questions at once. However, it would be a good idea to memorize some of these questions because they can be cues to help you follow communication and then assert yourself. As you practice these skills your goal is for the skills to become more automatic.

Learning to listen is an AD/HD student's most valuable tool! Yet, it is the most challenging. If you are an AD/HD student, you may not want to listen. You may want action and excitement because that is the way your brain is developed. You become bored in situations that most of us can easily tolerate. If you have AD/HD your brain gets satisfied in a different manner. Most of us can easily tolerate less thrill and excitement in our lives, both in our conversations and in our actions. Often, you may need more stimulation to have a feeling of being satisfied. This difficulty in satisfying yourself in your brain may be the reason why you engage in or can tolerate risk-taking behavior.

Do you want to be popular and have more friends? Then learn to observe and use your senses. Pay attention to what is going on right this minute. Use your eyes to focus more deeply on what you see. Take notice: observe how other students are acting. Watch how others present themselves. What is acceptable? Listen . . . deeply to what other students are saying. Listen for the pragmatics (i.e., the social language of speech) in conversations. What tone was used in the last sentence? What were they talking about in the conversation? Did the conversation mean something other than the words that were spoken? What was their facial expression or body language? Did these nonverbal (not verbal) signs of communication match their words? If not, why do you think that they did not? And, be aware of space. Are you too close to a student who has a 4 foot space cushion? Who likes for you to be close to them and hug them and who does not? Do you notice how a student or an adult's space cushion can change daily? Weekly? Hourly?

What are people wearing? What are other students talking about? How much do they talk about that subject? Listen for tone—when the conversation drops off, look for an opening to make a comment. Don't just blurt in over someone else's remarks. Wait your turn.

Impulsivity, inattention, and distractibility are all aspects that affect a student's ability to know how they feel. These issues interfere with an AD/HD student's ability to express what they feel. Why? Because their feelings may shift very rapidly. What an AD/HD student feels at 3:00 pm may not be what they feel at 3:05 pm. This can be a significant problem and can be quite confusing to others. It may also represent a wide range of different feelings rather than one particular feeling; this complex manner of having multiple feelings may be difficult to access and to express for an AD/HD student.

How to deal with this situation? The AD/HD adolescent may have to spend extra time in reviewing communication and coping strategies in order to be clearer about how they feel. They may need extra practice in learning and stating "I" messages. Of great importance is the awareness that their emotions can also be reflective of symptoms of AD/HD; i.e., that they feel a kaleidoscope of emotions, multiple emotions, and have significant difficulty sorting out what their true feelings are. In this case it may be wise to pick a couple of primary emotions and express them. For example: "I am upset about my grades and confused about why I scored poorly on the test." Also: "I feel I have been treated unfairly and I'm concerned about my privileges."

"I want to go out with Katie on Friday night, be with my cross country team, and go to the football game." An AD/HD student may feel equally passionate about all of the previous activities, and may have difficulty making decisions because all of it matters and it all has equal importance.

Impulsivity

Although impulsivity is a hallmark of AD/HD students, it is also an issue that all of us have difficulty with in our words and in our actions from time to time. Therefore, this issue will be given some extra attention. When you are impulsive, you speak or act without giving enough thought to your words or to your actions. You may not monitor your thoughts before they become words. You may forget to stop and think about the consequences of your actions.

Impulsive actions are less likely to happen when you use cause and effect. When you are impulsive, you don't plan. You make snap decisions and judgments. You go too fast. If you use **cause** and **effect** and **assertive skills**, you can reduce impulsivity in your life.

If you are in touch with your feelings and learn assertive skills, you can lessen your impulsive actions. Cause and effect minimizes impulsive actions. Decisions that are impulsive can lead to life changing consequences. To have sex on the spur of the moment is to not listen to the logic of "Will I get AIDS or other sexually transmitted diseases?" Other questions that a student can ask before having sex include:

- Am I creating a child?
- Will I be okay with myself in the morning?
- What do I truly want?
- Why am I doing this?
- What part of me is in charge at this moment?
- What do I need?

Other impulsive situations will come up that may have a less drastic effect on your life, but also need attention. I give this example about sex because it can have such powerful consequences. In truth, all of our actions lead to changes—both in us and in others. Practicing assertive skills with "I" messages makes you stop and think about your actions and the consequences.

To summarize, if you have AD/HD use these skills:

- **Stop** and **listen** to what is happening so you can identify what seems to be the real meaning of the conversation.
- **Identify** your feelings and locate what are your most important feelings.
- **Look** for cues and clues in conversations.
- **State** "I" messages.
- **Ask** for feedback from peers and adults whom you trust.

Learning Disabilities and Dyslexia

Learning differences can be manifest in many areas. Historically, the federal government has defined seven areas where learning disabilities can be exhibited. These seven areas include the following: basic reading skills, reading comprehension, mathematical calculation, mathematical reasoning, listening comprehension, written expression, and oral expression. Deficits in language based issues are defined in this book as dyslexia. The public may think of dyslexia as "reading words backward." In this book dyslexia is defined as difficulty with language, which includes problems with reading, writing, and spelling (*Lyon, Shaywitz, Shaywitz*, 2003).

There may be several issues that interfere with a student who has learning disabilities and his ability to define and express his feelings. Using assertive skills may be challenging. If a student has a language-based learning problem such as dyslexia, he may have difficulty organizing his words and clearly stating his thoughts and sentences. He may unknowingly express the opposite of what he is feeling. I have worked with dyslexic students who speak better when they are moving. To be able to move while you are speaking is not realistic for most students, and it may not be appropriate in most settings. How can a student deal with these issues? If a student has a learning difference, the need to express feelings and to be an advocate for himself may be more important than it would be for another student. Students who learn differently are likely to have difficulty in educational systems that do not "speak their language." In school they may suffer in silence if they can't speak up for themselves and alert their teachers as to how the curriculum needs to be modified to help them to succeed in their school work. Each learning problem needs to be clearly identified through a psychoeducational assessment. IDEA provides that students will be provided a free evaluation that assesses for learning and attentional problems. Behavior issues may also need to be investigated. As a result of the evaluation, a team of people meet to decide if the student qualifies for extra assistance or accommodations in the school setting. If the student exhibits "significant negative educational impact" as a result of the evaluation and the team findings, an IEP (Individualized Education Plan) or a 504 Plan will be developed.

First, it is important for you, the student, to be clear about your learning differences. Some questions that you need to be able to answer include the following:

- How are your learning differences expressed?
- What difficulties do you experience in the classroom?
- Do you have different problems in different classes; when are you most at risk for getting into trouble?
- How can you best speak up for yourself?
- How can you handle these issues with friends? With teachers and administrators?
- Are you able to successfully complete homework assignments (without significant stress)?

R U Assertive?

There are many educational interventions that may be necessary for a student who learns differently. For example, a student with a learning disability in written expression may need assistance in getting notes from class lectures. This student may need a peer note taker, a laptop, or copies of the teacher's notes.

A student with a math disability may need to turn his paper to the side and complete math problems with columns that naturally occur in the paper. This student may need math procedures broken into small, sequential steps. A student with a listening disability may need to sit near the front of the class, have the teacher produce a special "cue or signal" when a very important topic is being discussed, use a tape recorder, or have a peer note taker.

Perhaps these modifications are detailed in an IEP or in a 504 Plan that has been developed by the school and parents. However, teachers who have 150 students to teach every day may need assistance from the student who has learning differences to remind them of the student's accommodations and educational needs. In this situation, the student needs to be clear about his learning needs (acknowledge his learning differences) and be an advocate (a spokesperson) for himself. Ultimately, it is the student who needs to monitor his school work and take charge of his academic life. There are many parents who are excellent advocates for their children in educational settings. However, students should know their learning needs, and be primary spokespersons for themselves. As each student has clear knowledge of his learning differences, the student will be able to develop better self-knowledge. As I have already stated, self-knowledge is a first step in learning assertive skills. You can speak up for yourselves if you are clear about your educational needs. Your parents will not always be with you; it is your job to take control of being an advocate for yourself. These are good skills toward learning to be an advocate for yourself at school and these are good life skills. A student who is 15 years old and who is an advocate for himself in class will be able to navigate his college and work life with better confidence.

Examples of self-advocacy for the learning disabled student include the following:

- Asking for extra time on tests
- Requesting a different testing site
- Requesting instructions that are in bold print
- Asking for tests that are clearly readable
- Changing the format of tests (especially for a student who has a Nonverbal Learning Disorder)
- Utilizing assignment notebooks that are to be initialed by teachers, parents, and student
- Previewing homework assignments by the teacher and utilizing modifications based on the student and the type/severity of the learning problem
- Using books on tape
- Providing an extra copy of text books for home use
- Giving frequent access to drinking water and to bathrooms
- Making use of a laptop or an Alpha-Smart
- Using behavior management schedules
- Providing social skills training or individual counseling sessions
- Using reading material on the student's achievement, not ability level
- Utilizing a scribe (parent, teacher, tutor may transcribe assignments)
- Allowing electronic devices
- Providing assistance with organizational skills
- Utilizing preferential seating in the classroom
- Providing written instructions regarding class lectures and homework

R U Assertive?

The important aspect of accommodations is **not to make a student dependent on accommodations or avoidant of his responsibilities.** The most important feature is to put the student on an equal playing field with students who do not have learning challenges. In private practice, I push teenagers to be more independent, to work as hard as they can, and to overcome their learning differences. But, I would not ask a blind teenager to read printed text, or expect a deaf student to take notes during a verbal lecture. The learning differences I am referring to in this book may be more subtle—but can be destructive in interfering with a student's ability to experience success.

School is a student's job, and grades are a student's paycheck. We must support students in succeeding on their jobs and help them experience success through good work and study habits. Accommodations should never be conceived of as a crutch to avoid school work or to put forth less effort.

As you learn more about your learning differences use "I" messages and assertive skills to help you voice your needs at school and in life. In addition to the preceding recommendations remember that the basis of this book is that you must practice "I" messages and learn to speak for yourself. Practice "I" messages with a guidance counselor, a trusted adult, a friend, or a teacher. Ask for feedback about your efforts in being an advocate for yourself. Learn more about yourself. Learn a list of feeling words that will give you support in knowing yourself and in speaking up for yourself.

Here are some examples of "I" messages about being an advocate for yourself at school:

- I need to orally read this section in a private or quiet setting with only the teacher present.
- I need written instructions for this class lecture.
- How can I best study for the test since I am slow at taking notes in class?

Practice Exercises

Write out four "I" messages that you may use in school to be an advocate for yourself.

Nonverbal Learning Disorder (NLD)

Students with a Nonverbal Learning Disorder (NLD) have many good skills that assist them with their learning difference. Students with NLD usually have a rich vocabulary, they are often well read, and they have knowledge that may extend over a variety of topics. They typically have strong recall skills and can cite a storehouse of knowledge in many areas.

Students with nonverbal learning differences may have difficulty with large and fine motor skills, working with visual-spatial issues, and with social skills. Their fingers may be relatively slow in writing or executing their well-developed thoughts. They may have difficulty copying from the board, from their books, or from an overhead projector. NLD students may have difficulty with relationships—especially with relationships with students their age. Our most important form of communication is through our body, not with our words. In fact, communicating with our bodies is so important that research says that we communicate at least 65% of what we say with our bodies, not with words. Is that surprising? We "speak" with the way we shift our bodies, with our eyes, the way we turn our mouths, etc.

An NLD student needs assertive skills because the very nature of this learning difference suggests that the NLD student may be challenged with communication skills as well as with motor and visual-spatial abilities. Nonverbal communication is our body's way of "speaking," of communicating with others. Some positive aspects of body language may involve good eye contact, sitting up straight, speaking clearly, and using a tone that matches your words. Attention to your body and what it is communicating is essential. What is your face saying? Do you have a frown? A smile? Do you look confident? Tired? Overwhelmed?

The following traits outline some of the challenges that a student with a Nonverbal Learning Disorder (NLD) may exhibit:

1. **Gross and fine motor coordination:** With gross (large) motor coordination, an NLD student may be slow with large motor experiences: he may be slow to ride a bike, dress himself, throw a ball, or participate in sports. With fine motor coordination an NLD student may be challenged in using his hands/fingers for small motor tasks such as cutting and pasting, tying his shoes, writing with a pencil, coloring with crayons, etc. An NLD student may appear to be clumsy with motor skills, and may have issues with balance.

2. **Inability to "read" nonverbal communication; social skill "reading" deficits:** As previously noted, most of our communication is nonverbal. We communicate with our body more than we communicate with words. Therefore, "reading" others with nonwords is essential in good communication skills. An NLD

student may have trouble reading and responding accurately to nonverbal cues. An NLD student may miss or misinterpret gestures. This student may become overwhelmed when there are quick changes in communication or if there is more than one conversation that is going on.

3. **Visual-spatial integration concerns:** Visual-spatial skills indicate how you see and arrange objects around you, and how you relate to space. Some people have well developed visual-spatial skills such as an architect or a surgeon. An interior designer can manipulate space in his mind and then make it become a reality with furniture, paint, fabric, etc. An NLD student is challenged with these concepts. An NLD student may have trouble perceiving and making modifications to the space around him or in his head. For example, an NLD student whom I saw for years in private practice moved his place of residence during the course of therapy. For at least a year he would ask his Mom on the way home if they were close to his house. Usually, they would be a few houses away from his house when he asked where he was in location to his home. It took this student approximately 1 1/2 years to begin to get comfortable with the new visual-spatial field of his neighborhood and begin to recognize what might have readily been a familiar sight to another student.

Another example of a student with NLD difficulties involved the following: I evaluated a high school junior at a boarding school who was a fine football player. However, he had mild symptoms of NLD. His coach called me one day and said that Sam was a great player as long as the play/set was predictable. Coach said that when something unpredictable happened on the field that "Sam is lost." That was true because Sam had trouble "reading the field" and predicting the next move. He performed quite well as long as he could relate to and predict plays. When a very unpredictable play happened on the field, the student lost his bearings and had trouble responding. It was as though Sam was two different players; this could be explained by his symptoms of NLD.

The student with NLD presents many challenges in learning assertive skills. The very nature of an NLD reflects that the student will have a good vocabulary and a storehouse of words. The problem that this student encounters lies more in interpreting nonverbal cues (remember, at least 65% of communication is nonverbal). Therefore, the NLD student who struggles in interpreting "non-words" misses the subtle cues in conversation. This means that the student may misjudge the place or way to respond and is more likely to miss subtle cues that may have directed him regarding how to respond as well as when to respond. The NLD student may miss another student's sharp turned head, wink, raised eyebrow, frown, etc. This inability to "read" a situation can lead to much difficulty at school, with peers, at home with family members, etc.

The NLD student may frequently feel "lost" in conversations with peers. He may compensate by relating to and talking to adults or to younger students. He may develop "adult-like" behavior, and miss out on connecting to his peers in appropriate social-emotional situations.

For the NLD student, dealing with these situations through the use of verbal questions is a good approach. One of the biggest assets that an NLD student has is a rich storehouse of words. In situations where an NLD student is not clear, he should use this powerful strength to help him understand and interact in more favorable ways. Clear up what is going on in the conversation by asking questions. What were you saying? Did you ask me something? What was your last comment? In this manner an NLD student is asking if his hunch or perception of the conversation is accurate. However, it can be embarrassing to question a peer group that is fast-paced and has a level of social-emotional expectation exceeding the level to which an NLD student can track and respond. In addition to verbal questions, learning to read faces, actual instruction in body language, a stronger awareness of space cushions, etc. helps to bridge the gap between guessing and knowing how to read others and responding to the body language of others.

Another intervention that works includes spending time learning to "read" what is challenging with peers and others. Practice at home with family, in therapy, in counseling, and with close friends who are aware of your difficulty in "reading situations." Peer feedback is powerful. Ask a teacher who is familiar with you and with NLD to watch how you interact with others and give you feedback and suggestions. Or, if you can get peer feedback in a "safe" setting (i.e., a group therapy or a social skills group) you will benefit from this approach. Another strategy that works is verbal self-direction. Guide yourself through challenging situations by talking to yourself inside and providing a verbal roadmap. See Chapter 7 for more information on Self-Talk. And, remember to use assertive skills in tracking where you are and how you want to respond.

Also, it is very important to make good use of the NLD's student's rich vocabulary. Once an NLD student learns when and what to verbalize, he is often "in his element" discussing interesting topics.

Most importantly, don't be passive. Don't sit on the sidelines and fear involvement because of lack of comfort in the situation. Use "I" messages to state how you feel, what direction you prefer the group to go in, what skills you can provide, etc.

It is important to remember that the NLD student wants to belong, to be accepted by his peers—just like other students. An NLD student may come across as being more self-focused and self-involved than other students. However, this is one of the symptoms of NLD, and it is not an accurate assessment. Also, while the child is young, an NLD student's parents usually develop high expectations for this student because NLD students begin their education with strong verbal skills. They usually make outstanding grades in elementary school. Middle school years may witness a drop-off in grades. As the school curriculum becomes more intuitive—in middle and high school years—there is a greater demand for organizational skills, written production, time management, etc. By middle school years an NLD student may begin to show signs of academic challenges, grades may drop, and social expectations may falter. This situation may be more challenging because the parents initially had such high expectations for their NLD child. Interventions and assertive skills are essential in helping an NLD student navigate the increasing challenges of school and life.

Chapter 6
Extreme Social Situations
Bullying, Teasing, and Shyness

Bullying and Teasing

Most teenagers are easy to get along with, but there is a very small portion of the teenage population that defines itself by its inappropriate behavior. Students with inappropriate behavior may communicate through bullying, teasing, and intimidating other students. You will benefit from learning to identify which students are good for you to associate with and those who may cause you emotional hurt or harm. In this chapter you will learn techniques for dealing with students who have bullying or intimidating behavior.

Also, there are students who may be challenged in utilizing assertive skills because they are shy. A shy student who is reading this book may identify with the knowledge that he may have assertive skills, but he may be challenged in using these skills because of his shyness. This chapter will give a "push" to those students to begin using assertive skills and to become better advocates for themselves.

Bullying and teasing occur when another student makes fun of you, puts you down, or acts as if he is in a place of authority over you. It is important to realize that bullying and teasing often comes from insecurity in the person who is using those tactics.

R U Assertive?

The student who is unkind enough to tease another student may have feelings of insecurity and inadequacy that may not be realized or resolved. A bully may have been raised in a household where aggression, dominance, and "put-downs" were used as a way of communicating or of controlling another person. It is much like the personality that you would expect to find in a dictator.

Teasing may involve making good fun of another person in a playful manner that is not harmful. Or, teasing may involve unkind or cruel remarks to another student that are intended to hurt or to cause harm. Sometimes students say hurtful things in order to separate themselves from other students, to feel more important about themselves. In this situation the student may develop a false sense of being better than someone else. This type of teasing is an unhealthy way of getting needs met. There are situations when teasing is appropriate and can lift a mood, but if you use teasing to cause harm to another person or to elevate yourself, you have been aggressive and, perhaps, abusive. If you feel good about yourself, then you will not feel OK about tolerating hurtful remarks about yourself.

Assertive skills and "I" messages are good techniques to use in dealing with bullying and teasing behaviors. Bullies are often puzzled by a student who has enough strength to say:

- I feel picked on.
- I don't like being called that name.
- I don't know if you realize that your remarks are hurtful.
- I can find an adult to help us with us with this.

All of these remarks put another student on notice that you have emotional strength, that you are clear about "your ground," and that you have worth. If you realize that you have worth, you will speak up for yourself and assert yourself—because you

Extreme Social Situations

deserve to be treated better, and this is one way of taking care of yourself.

Also, there can be strength in walking away. There may be situations where you assert yourself by removing yourself from the situation.

Students have told me that when being confronted by a bully there are times when they don't feel that their words carry enough weight—they feel that they must fight or defend themselves in a more physical than verbal manner. In this situation, put more effort into taking care of yourself with the strength of your words. Make your words and the strength of your body become as one. Use a serious voice and let the words that you speak bring strength and power into your life. Stand straight and erect with your legs slightly apart when you speak. If you are sitting down, sit with your back very straight and erect, like there is a board behind it. Do not crouch down. Use your body to convey strength. Say your words with force; you can speak assertively. Give this a try. There is always a first time; try this new skill. It may seem odd at first for you to act and speak in a bold manner, but give yourself permission to speak up. Don't sound like a mouse in the presence of a lion—speak loudly enough and with strength to get your message across. Remember that **the way** or **the manner** in which you speak is as powerful as what you speak.

Research states that if one student "sticks up" for another student who is being bullied, then peers will not join in with the bully. They will back away. Therefore, be sensitive to other students in regard to this issue about bullying. Be on the lookout for peers who may be in trouble and perhaps your words and presence can have power for the student who is being bullied. There may come a time when a student that you stood up for takes up for you.

And know that once you have stood up to a bully, whether for yourself or for a peer, you have in some way benefited all other students who may be victims or who may be bullied. Your assertive skills can benefit many students. Your growth and development in some way touches all students.

R U Assertive?

Practice Exercises

How would you handle the following situations?

What would you do if students at school called you aggressive or hurtful names and put you down?

___

What would you do if a gang of students bullied you in the parking lot before or after school?

___

What would you do if a bully tried to pick a fight with you?

___

Extreme Social Situations

What would you do if a bully picked on you in front of someone who you cared about or thought was important?

_____

_____

_____

_____

Shy

The issues as written in this book are more complicated for a student who is shy. Shy students struggle with self-advocacy. Often they are aware of their feelings, but to speak up is emotionally painful; it is better to be in pain than to go forward and endure the greater pain of speaking up. Shy students may not feel confident. For students who are shy, I ask them to work in stages, to take small steps, and to be patient with themselves. Practice "I" messages at home with and without a mirror. You can practice "I" messages in your bedroom or in a bathroom. That's right. Close the bathroom door and look at yourself in the mirror and practice "I" messages. Do this until you are comfortable, until it becomes more natural for you. Practice "I" messages with your dog, cat, or hamster. Try to persist. In life, try these exercises in a few situations. If there are four opportunities for assertive skills, use "I" messages on at least one occasion. Then reward yourself. If you are shy, when you speak up for yourself, you have accomplished something significant, and you need to reward yourself. The reward does not have to involve money—perhaps you can have a friend over, watch an extra TV program, etc. Or, you may want to reward yourself with a new CD, a shirt, or a trip to the movies, etc.

We are not born assertive and we cannot learn to be assertive all at once. It is true that some students naturally have more assertive skills than other students. However, even if you are assertive, additional practice will help you develop and sharpen your skills. If you are not naturally assertive, these skills will help you develop your ability to speak up for yourself and take care of yourself. Being assertive is a skill that you can aspire to at any time. Take a step in learning assertive skills. Then there will be another step and another step. Taking small steps helps you grow as a person and reminds you that you have strength and courage. You will grow in your ability to be aware of your feelings and in your skills in being able to state your wants and needs.

Practice Exercises

Try some of the following exercises to help you overcome some of your symptoms of shyness:

- Make an effort to speak to someone new at school each day.
- Try to attend a new club or social event.
- Count how many students you talk to outside of class in a school day. Slowly increase that number.
- Invite a student over to your house or to an activity outside of school.

Chapter 7
Additional Self-Support Techniques

In addition to learning assertive skills there are other techniques that will support you as you learn more meaningful ways of taking care of yourself. This chapter will expose you to four techniques of self-care that can strengthen your assertive skills. The techniques in this chapter are additional ways of taking care of yourself. They are techniques that can be used in addition to your assertive skills and "I" messages. The techniques used with Fogging, Broken Record, Positive Self-Talk, and Positive Pictures in your Mind will give you an extra push or support in speaking up for yourself and in taking care of yourself. Exercises for developing each skill are included.

Fogging

Fogging is a great technique that allows you to go with the flow of what is going on in order to sidestep a confrontation that may be hurtful to you. By using Fogging techniques you disarm the person who is attacking you with their words. The purpose of Fogging is to "go with the flow." If you are hurt by someone's comments—do not let them know this. You can lessen their hurtful remarks by not meeting their words with resistance. In martial arts this concept is called aikido. Use your strength to quietly by-pass your opponent.

These are examples of Fogging:

When a student says to you	You might respond by saying
Your hair is standing straight out...	I thought that was the style.
Your clothes are old-fashioned—can't you afford new clothes?	Old is in, you need to look at what you wear.
You're so small, I can beat you up with one hand...	I know... that's why I am out of here
You are a preppy, rich kid...	I know... I wish my family had less money
You're a snob and you think you're so popular...	I am a little bit cooler than you.

Practice Exercises

When a student says to you, "You're too dumb to pass algebra..." You might respond by saying:

___

___

When a student says to you, "Your parents treat you like a baby..." You might respond by saying:

___

___

Additional Self-Support Techniques

When a student says to you, "He's only dating you because your dad is rich..."
You might respond by saying:

_____

_____

When a student says to you, "You're so ugly I don't know how you are able to leave your house..."
You might respond by saying:

_____

_____

Broken Record

My clients rarely know what I am talking about when I use the phrase "Broken Record." When I was growing up, we all had record players, and our music was played with albums on record players. When the record got a scratch on it, you heard the same lines over and over and over. That's because the record was "stuck" and would not go any further. This is where the term "Broken Record" originated. The same concept is true for taking care of yourself and in using assertive skills. In assertive skills teachings you may need to apply the concept of Broken Record to your words. If you are not being heard, you may need to state the same words over and over . . . until your message has been acknowledged or received. The secret to Broken Record is to stay with the story line, even if you feel a little silly by repeating yourself over and over.

For example, a tape player that I purchased a few years ago worked for only a few days. It then broke. I took it back to the store, with the receipt in hand. The clerk at the store said that I did not have a warranty. I stated that I had purchased the tape player that very week, and that through no fault of mine, it was not working. The clerk would not return my money or give me a new tape player. I respectfully asked to speak to someone in authority over the clerk. I kept saying the same story over and over, not departing from the story line. I left the store with a new tape player. I received a new tape player because I was not moveable with my words. I played Broken Record with my words. I was convinced of my right to receive a piece of equipment that worked and I stayed with the truth of the events. Part of being able to utilize the concept of Broken Record is having a conviction about what you are trying to accomplish, believing that you can stay with the story, and not deviate from it. Stay with the topic—*do not drift!*

Now, as a teenager, one of your greatest strengths is verbally wearing your parents down. You know that you have won many an argument based on outlasting your parents. Do not use Broken Record to get your way if your intent is one of selfish desire. Use Broken Record to take care of yourself, assert yourself, and be an advocate for yourself. Use Broken Record when you may have been wronged or mistreated— use Broken Record for honorable reasons in taking care of yourself.

What are some situations where you can use Broken Record? How could Broken Record be useful in these situations?

If other students want to skip math class and go to Burger King. . . you can use Broken Record by saying:

- I need to take notes in class today.
- I need to take my own notes in class today.
- I need to learn about variables in math class today.
- I need to get clear about homework assignments in math. I'd better not miss class today.

In this exercise the student stayed with the idea of "being in class." In this situation it was the "staying in class" that was purposeful and important.

Additional Self-Support Techniques

Practice Exercises

Write out two examples of using Broken Record when you have been asked to go to an activity that your parents will not allow you to attend.

_____

_____

_____

_____

_____

_____

Write out an example of Broken Record when you're asked to cheat on an exam.

_____

_____

_____

_____

_____

_____

Write out an example of Broken Record when you are asked to use drugs.

_____

_____

_____

_____

R U Assertive?

Write out an example of Broken Record when you want to understand why your science grade is so low.

_____

_____

_____

Write out an example of Broken Record when someone asks to take some of your Adderall.

_____

_____

_____

Positive Self-Talk

Positive Self-Talk are positive statements that we make in our mind that significantly influence our mood, our behavior, and our future. Dr. David Burns in his book *Ten Days to Self-Esteem* (1993) states that you feel the way that you think. Therefore, our thoughts are powerful and need to be watched. Learn to observe your thoughts. First, notice what you are telling yourself. What words do you speak in your mind about yourself? About others? Do you compare yourself to others? How do you stack up? What do you say about yourself? Are your thoughts negative? i.e., do you say something like: "she'll never go out with me; I'm too dumb to take that course; they'll never include me in their group." Negative thoughts are a way of putting yourself down and holding yourself back. You may become what your thoughts speak to you.

Are you able to think positive thoughts such as the following:

Additional Self-Support Techniques

"I like the way I completed that Spanish project. I did a good job on my math homework. I am going to run for Student Council and win." etc.

After listening to your internal conversations do you feel encouraged? Ready to tackle a new project? or Do you have more enthusiasm?

or

Do you feel defeated, discouraged, and ready to quit? If so, then your words to yourself have taken you to a place where you are your own worst enemy. You have defeated yourself with your words, and perhaps this was accomplished even before you began your task. Choose to give yourself support and strength with your words. Be specific in your Self-Talk in how you define what you want and what would need to happen for your thoughts to become a reality.

There are times when we are all uncertain. We can "own" our anxiety and concerns and still be positive about the future. One of my clients who was challenged in learning martial arts developed these positive Self-Talk statements to help him as he acquired new skills:

- This is a new skill for me and I can be patient with myself while I am learning it.
- I am a good, smart student, and I can do many things well.
- I am proud that I have made progress in this area.
- I am a talented and wonderful person.
- I am just learning this skill and my abilities will improve.
- I will receive all of the help that I need from others to learn this new skill.
- This new skill is emerging in me.

My client made flash cards with these statements, and he reviewed them every week. When he felt less than up to the challenge, he remembered the positive Self-Talk in his mind and was able to deal with the task. Be specific with your positive Self-Talk. Work on substituting a positive or encouraging thought for negative self-talk and cultivate positive words in your mind.

Practice Exercises

Write out two positive Self-Talk statements when you are worried about asking someone to a school dance.

___

___

___

___

___

Write out two positive Self-Talk statements when you are concerned about trying out for the basketball team.

___

___

___

___

___

Additional Self-Support Techniques

Write out two positive Self-Talk statements when you have decided to run for student council.

_____

_____

_____

_____

_____

Write out two positive Self-Talk statements when you are discouraged about studying for your math exam.

_____

_____

_____

_____

_____

Perhaps one of the best Self-Talk statements comes from the song with the jingle "Don't Worry, Be Happy." If you cannot think of positive Self-Talk just remember that phrase.

Positive Pictures in Your Mind

In addition to having a better awareness of your words, it is a good idea to think about what pictures you form in your mind. What kind of pictures do you daily picture in your mind? Are these pictures negative or positive images? Do you see yourself as popular, surrounded by many friends, as making good grades, as being healthy and strong? Or do you see yourself flying down the road in a fast car breaking the speed limit, smoking cigarettes, using drugs, or being alone? Is there a difference between how you see yourself and how you really are? Would you like to change the pictures? You can.

Do you see yourself growing in your assertive skills? Learning to speak up for yourself? Can you picture yourself as a winner? Can you picture yourself as someone who can tackle challenging projects and succeed? The pictures that you form in your mind may influence the outcome in which you are involved.

Many of the athletes that I see in private practice have learned how to develop and keep positive pictures of themselves in the sport in which they are involved. If you are a swimmer, do you see yourself touching the time block before the other swimmers? Do you see yourself cutting time off of the clock? Reaching your PR (i.e., personal record)?

You can use these same visualization skills to see yourself as a winner with assertive skills. In your mind's eye, picture yourself speaking up to a classmate that you found intimidating. See yourself speaking to a teacher about a grade that was not satisfactory. Picture yourself asking your parents if you can drive their car to a special event. Picture yourself asking a special girl out on a date. See yourself doing these activities, in vivid colors in your mind with much success. Believe in yourself. Picture good things and bring them into your life.

Practice Exercises

Where are you most challenged in your life right now? What positive pictures can you develop in your mind to help you with these challenges?

___

What positive pictures do you need to develop in your mind to assist you with your school work?

___

What positive pictures do you need to develop in your mind to help you with your relationship to your boyfriend, to a girlfriend?

___

R U Assertive?

What positive pictures do you need to develop in your mind to be more popular?

_____

_____

_____

_____

What positive pictures do you need to develop in your mind to help you compete for the drama club?

_____

_____

_____

_____

Conflict Management

Conflict is a natural part of the process of life. Conflict can be described as two opposing forces that do not agree. It is how we handle conflict, how we deal with conflict that makes it a problem, a challenge, or an opportunity for growth.

Conflict can be a chance for growth and positive change. Many students are afraid of conflict. Perhaps you were raised in a house where conflict was not acceptable. There may have been tension in your household; words may not have been spoken, but you felt an atmosphere that was heavy and tense. Did you keep silent? How did you handle the unspoken tension? Did you pretend that it was not there? Or, at the other extreme, do you live in a house where there is significant shouting and conflict. Maybe family members do not monitor their thoughts—they just shout them out. You may have grown up very comfortable with conflict, hostility, and tension, as if it were a natural occurrence in your life. You may create conflict because you are comfortable with it.

Let's Explore Conflict:

First, you need to figure out how you *feel* about conflict.

- Are you comfortable when you are in a situation that causes conflict?
- What is it about the conflict that "pushes your buttons"?
- What is it that makes you feel uncomfortable?
- What is it that makes you want to run away or act out?
- What is it that makes you want to attack or hurt another person (with words) when you are in conflict?
- Do you want to "ramp up" the heat when you are in conflict?

If you are having trouble finding your true feelings in a situation where there is conflict or where you feel conflicted, go back to Chapter 3 and explore your feelings with writing sprints, drawing, relaxation exercises, etc.

Now that you are clearer about how you feel about conflict, let us examine some responses to conflict. Choose which response reflects you. Consider if you are responding with feelings or with behavior:

- Do you shy away or avoid situations that involve conflict? (a passive response)
- Do you often become angry when you are in conflict? (perhaps an aggressive response)
- Do you avoid conflict for the moment and then try to seek revenge or hurt the person later? (a passive-aggressive response)
- Do you deal with conflict in the present moment by stating your feelings and making appropriate "I" statements? (an assertive response)

- Are you willing to look at yourself and state your position clearly? (an assertive response)
- Who in your family deals with conflict like you do?

Do not think that conflict is going to just disappear. Resist the urge to get out your magic wand and pretend that this is a Cinderella story, that things can be fixed with a magic wand and all will be well.

Conflict is a potential growth exercise for you. Let's explore some concepts to keep in mind when you are in conflict. It is very important to use your "I" messages when you are in conflict. Remember, state your position clearly. "I" messages give clarity and help you to "own" how you feel and your desired outcome. Stay with the topic. Do not bring up "old wounds" or other unresolved topics. Use "Broken Record" (Chapter 7) if you need help staying on topic. Do not attack or put down the person with whom you are in conflict. Realize that you may create your feelings in others. For example, if you are in conflict with a teacher, you may be angry and upset. You may create those same feelings in the teacher with whom you are trying to resolve the conflict. You may also create your feelings in your parents, your boyfriend, or anyone else with whom you are trying to resolve the conflict in a situation. Try to monitor your emotions. If you do not stay in control of yourself, emotions may take over and you may not resolve the situation.

Find common ground. Is there a path that you and the person with whom you are in conflict can agree? If you can agree on one part of the conflict, you can begin to build a solution, a bridge. Then, ask yourself, "What type of ending do I want?" In other words, you might consider "working backwards" in your thoughts. Perhaps you can "see" a successful outcome in your mind, or you can "hear" the words to a script that will be a good ending. These techniques may help you find a successful outcome.

Seek support from others. Perhaps you and the person with whom you are in conflict can agree to seek a neutral person (i.e., guidance counselor, therapist, etc.) or someone to help the two of you seek a solution.

Additional Self-Support Techniques

State the other person's position. So often, we do not understand what another person is requesting or truly wants. Listen. Find clarity.

Conflict Management Suggestions

- Use "I" messages
- Stay with the topic
- Listen
- Do not attack or put down
- Realize that you may create your feelings in someone else (therefore, monitor your feelings)
- Use the "Broken Record" technique
- Find common ground (points you and the other person can agree on)
- In your mind develop the ending that you want
- Seek support
- Ask questions
- Restate the other person's opinion

Thoughts About Conflict

List two situations where you have recently had conflict.

_____

_____

_____

_____

R U Assertive?

How did you handle the conflict in these situations?

What could you do to improve your conflict management skills?

Who in your life manages conflict well?

Additional Self-Support Techniques

Who in your life manages conflict poorly?

___
___
___
___
___
___

Conclusion

One of the biggest problems that we face today, not only in America, but in our world, is the problem of self-interest. If you think about it, if we could only get beyond ourselves, the world would be a much better place. Perhaps this is more difficult than it appears to be. With assertive skills, I am asking you to get to know yourself better, to speak up for yourself, to be an advocate for yourself. This is not a form of self-focusing, but it is a form of self-advocacy. Once you get the hang of knowing yourself and being a spokesperson for yourself, then your next mission is to be a spokesperson for others. Speak up for the student at school who is ignored or bullied. Say "Hi" to someone that you never speak to. Include a shy student at your lunch table. Go out of your way to be friendly to a teacher or to an administrator. Offer to be involved in service projects. Look for ways to contribute to your world.

In this book I hope that you have found ways to speak up for yourself, to take care of your wants and your needs. You have the ability to send yourself the message, "I count. What I think and feel matters." No two snowflakes are alike, and there is no one on this planet who is like you. You are unique. You are worthy. You must use your voice—first to take care of yourself—and then, secondly, to be a spokesperson for all. The good that you do for yourself matters, just as every act of kindness and goodness to another student or to any other human being matters.

I shall close this book with a quote from the Jewish sage Hillel which I hope becomes part of your life as you practice assertive skills:

> "If I am not for myself, who will be for me?
> If I am for myself only, what am I?
> If not now, when?"

Additional Practice Exercises

Using what you have learned about yourself and assertive skills, how will you deal with these situations?

1. Your best friend doesn't invite you to her sleepover.

2. Your teacher has given you a low grade for your English paper.

3. You overhear your mom and dad fighting and you're worried they might separate or divorce.

4. Your best friend needs a higher math grade to graduate and asks to look on your paper at the exam.

R U Assertive?

5. You want to have the singing role in the class play, but are afraid to try out for the part.

6. Your brother is frequently in your room, messing with your things.

7. You feel that no matter how hard you try your work is not good enough.

8. The kids you used to hang around with are ignoring you this year.

9. Your boyfriend says that you need to prove that you love him and to do this you must have sex with him.

In each of these situations identify the problem, create solutions and develop assertive skills.

Identify the Problem

Additional Practice Exercises

Design Solutions

Assertive Skills Response

Identify the Problem

Design Solutions

Assertive Skills Response

R U Assertive?

Identify the Problem

_____
_____
_____

Design Solutions

_____
_____
_____

Assertive Skills Response

_____
_____
_____

Identify the Problem

_____
_____
_____

Design Solutions

_____
_____
_____

Additional Practice Exercises

Assertive Skills Response

Identify the Problem

Design Solutions

Assertive Skills Response

Self-Knowledge Practice Exercises

What do you want most for your life right now?

Right now in your life, what has the most priority?

Where does your attention go?

What do you not care about?

Additional Practice Exercises

Do you feel that you assert your opinions?

What are your rights?

What are the rights of others?

What is the difference between what you want and what your teachers/parents want?

R U Assertive?

What does your coach expect of you?

_____
_____
_____
_____

What do your parents expect of you?

_____
_____
_____
_____

What do other students want/expect of you?

_____
_____
_____
_____

Remember, being aware of how you feel may not be easy!

Additional Practice Exercises

What jobs have you thought about?

What steps will carry you to your goals?

What would you like to say to your parents if you knew that you would not get in trouble?

What would you like to tell your brother or sister if you did not have to monitor your words?

R U Assertive?

What would you like to tell your math teacher?

_____

_____

_____

_____

What would you like to tell your principal or your guidance counselor?

_____

_____

_____

_____

Ask yourself these questions to learn more about you, so that you can be more assertive:

What have you done today that you feel good about?

_____

_____

_____

_____

Additional Practice Exercises

What have you done that makes you feel sad?

To whom would you like to give a hug?

Who have you thanked today?

When have you shown an attitude of gratitude?

Who have you hurt today?

___

What feelings went unnoticed by you until now?

___

How were you assertive?

___

References

American Psychiatric Association. 2000. *Diagnostic and Statistical Manual of Mental Disorders*, fourth edition, American Psychiatric Association, Washington, D.C.

Borysenko, J. 1990. *Guilt is the Teacher, Love is the Lesson.* New York: Warner Books, Inc.

Burns, D. 1993. *Ten Days to Self-Esteem.* New York: Harper Collins.

Federal Register. 2005. Assistance to States for the Education of Children with Disabilities; Preschool Grants for Children with Disabilities; and Service Obligations Under Special Education—Personnel development to Improve Service and Results for Children with Disabilities. Department of Education. CFR Parts 300, 301, and 304. January 21, 2005, Part II.

Lyon, G. R., Shaywitz, S. E., & Shaywitz, B. A. 2003. A Definition of Dyslexia. *Annals of Dyslexia*, 53, 1-14.

McKay, M., and Rogers, P. 2000. *The Anger Control Workbook.* Oakland, CA.: New Harbinger Publications.

Weil, A. 1999. *Breathing The Master Key to Self Healing Study Guide.* Boulder, CO.: Sounds True.

About the Author

Gloria Hash Marcus is a Licensed PsychoEducational Specialist, a Licensed Professional Counselor, and Nationally Certified School Psychologist who has forty years of experience working with children, adolescents, and adults. Ms. Marcus has extensive experience in school systems, having served as an administrator, school psychologist, consultant, and teacher. Ms. Marcus' broad-based background with children and adolescents includes work in a developmental pediatric clinic, in a psychiatric hospital, and in a state mental health agency.

Ms. Marcus' areas of expertise include assessment and treatment of learning disabilities, dyslexia, Nonverbal Learning Disorders, and Attention-Deficit/Hyperactivity Disorder (AD/HD).

Specialty areas include treatment for depression; anxiety and stress; and development of healthy parenting strategies. In addition to working with children, adolescents, and families in a private practice, she lectures nationally on Multiple Intelligences and Assertive Skills. Ms. Marcus develops curricula for Multiple Intelligences that are specific to school settings. She has taught Multiple Intelligences for years at private schools.

Ms. Marcus conducts psychoeducational evaluations investigating the cognitive, academic, social, and processing needs of children, adolescents, and adults.

Her current practice location is Halsey Counseling and Educational Center: www.halseycounseling.com